THE JOY OF KEEPING SCORE

THE JOY OF KEEPING SCORE

*How Scoring the Game Has Influenced
and Enhanced the History of Baseball*

Paul Dickson

A HARVEST BOOK

HARCOURT BRACE & COMPANY

San Diego   New York   London

This Harvest edition published by arrangement with Walker and Company.

Library of Congress Cataloging-in-Publication Data
Dickson, Paul.
The joy of keeping score: how scoring the game has influenced
and enhanced the history of baseball/Paul Dickson.—1st Harvest ed.
p.   cm.—(A Harvest book)
Originally published: New York: Walker, 1996.
Includes bibliographical references and index.
ISBN 0-15-600516-6
1. Baseball—Scorekeeping.   I. Title.
[GV879.D54   1997]
796.357'021—dc21   97-14100

Book design by Ron Monteleone
Printed in the United States of America
First Harvest edition 1997
A C E F D B

For when the one great Scorer comes

   To write against your name,

He'll write not that you won or lost,

   But how you played the game.

                         —GRANTLAND RICE, 1908

YOU CAN'T TELL THE PLAYERS WITHOUT A SCORECARD.

                      —TRADITIONAL CRY OF SCORECARD VENDORS

ontents

THE JOY OF KEEPING SCORE

INTRODUCTION

For when the one great Scorer comes
To write against your name,
He marks—not that you won or lost—
But how did that last guy go out?

–JOHN DREBINGER
OF THE *NEW YORK TIMES* AFTER ANOTHER REPORTER
ASKED HIM HOW A PLAY HAD GONE

*T*he world is divided into two kinds of baseball fans: those who keep score at the ballgame . . . and those who have never made the leap. The book now in your hands is for both kinds. It will tell the reader how to score, explain the various systems, illuminate the sublime glories of scoring, and open a window on baseball's history you may not have looked through before.

The real reason I've written this book is simple enough: to bring the man, woman, or child in the stands or in front of the television back into a game that seems, at its highest level, to have turned its back on the fans.

Scoring *is* the fan's game. It does *not* belong to the owners, players, their union, or Major League Baseball. It is literally ours. There is a small irony here, which is that the people who actually play and manage the game are the game and, therefore, have no need to score it. Vast numbers of players, certainly the majority, have never scored a game.

Scoring *is* the fan's game primarily because it is enjoyable and useful at any level on which fans watch or participate: the majors or minors; Little League; fantasy games; organized softball—in every instance allowing you to re-create a game days, weeks, even years later. Scoring will always bring you closer to the game on the field, giving you an understanding you cannot gain otherwise. I daresay you'll appreciate the game all the

Rabid bleacherites at the Polo Grounds in April, 1938. Mostly male and wearing hats, this crew displays a deep interest in scorekeeping. (National Baseball Library, Cooperstown, N.Y.)

2

3

more, which may be important to restoring your enjoyment in the wake of the strike of August 1994.

So get a [baseball] life and score!

The idea for this book came in March 1989 when, through an odd bit of good fortune, I ended up in the broadcasting booth with Red Sox radio broadcaster Joe Castiglione announcing a spring training game against the Houston Astros. (His regular partner had left midgame with a toothache, and I, who had been in the booth for a pregame interview about a book I had written, was asked to fill in.)

Other than the fact that I was living out an adult fantasy, what impressed me most about the event was that Castiglione had total recall of every detail from the early innings of the game, relying on nothing more sophisticated

Joe Castiglione's scorecard that inspired the author to write this book. (Spring Training, 1989)

Press box at the 1911 World Series. Then as now, the press box houses the official scorer as well as reporters who keep their own score. (National Baseball Library, Cooperstown, N.Y.)

than a preprinted form with marks and numbers on it.

For years, I had imagined that radio and television play-by-play broadcasters sat in front of a computer monitor on which all this information was displayed in sentence form. Imagined, too, were a couple of young folks offstage entering every pitch of each at bat into the system. How else could you recall in the eighth exactly what had happened in the first inning and run through the game an inning at a time at the end of the game?

When Castiglione finished his final recap he unceremoniously threw away the piece of paper. Chucked it. I picked it up, spent about five minutes deciphering his code, and realized that in a computerized, realtime age I was looking at a nineteenth-century system that was at once idiosyncratic, creative, useful, and without flaw. From that point on, I began collecting all that I could on scoring systems and the baseball history they represent.

Though I came to serious scoring late, it was clearly in my blood. My great-grandfather, Philip Lehrbach, who among other

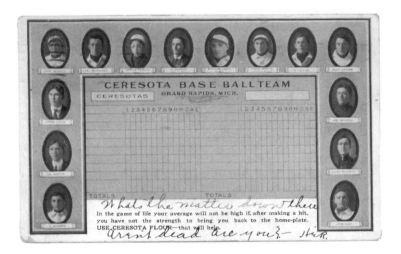

things was a business partner of Charles Ebbets, was an avid scorer and the first human I had ever watched score a game from the radio. My father was not a scorer, but he had a good reason. As a young entrepreneur he had sold ads in scorecards that he had planned to give away outside the Polo Grounds in New York. He was quickly stopped by representatives of the stadium concessionaire. A few days later he was back to offer a free scorecard, with ads, in the form of a fan with a handle, but this apparently ran afoul of an ordinance that for some reason prohibited giving away useful things for nothing in front of the park. My dad took me to dozens of baseball games, but he never scored and, predictably, we did not go to the Polo Grounds. Sad to say, I was scorecard-deprived until 1989, the year I turned fifty.

Meanwhile, the art of scoring has evolved since Henry Chadwick published the first baseball scorecard and box-scoring system adopted by organized baseball in 1863. Rule changes have altered scoring techniques, and as you will see, any number of fascinating, often intricate, scoring systems and embellishments have been devised. But as veteran broadcaster Chuck Thompson, long associated with the Baltimore Orioles, proudly says of himself and his colleagues: "We all still use the old-fashioned, hand-operated scorecard. All of us."

1 **WHY SCORE?**

"Keeping score is merely improving opportunity. The fan who
fails to do it misses half the game. Most spectators watch a
great play with an interest which, however intense, is forgot-
ten in the thriller of the next inning. They leave the grounds
with a hazy idea of a rather enjoyable afternoon, whose main fea-
tures are scarce refreshed by reading the press accounts of them some hours later.
Keeping score remedies all this. It burns the play into memory. It greatly
increases the spectator's knowledge of the game. It increases to just that degree
his pleasure in watching a contest. And, best of all, it is a pleasure in itself, not
the disagreeable thing it seems. A few simple rules, practice—and keeping score
becomes second nature to the fan."

–C. P. STACK,
BASEBALL MAGAZINE, MAY 1914, FROM HIS ARTICLE TITLED
"THE PLEASURE AND PROFIT OF KEEPING SCORE"

The urge to score is as old as the game itself and borrows significantly from the book-keeping instincts of British cricketeers. Early engravings of baseball games show official scorers in chairs along the first-base line. Fans scored from the early days as well, and many different systems emerged—some of which were so informal as to be lost to the twentieth century. As early as 1874 Henry Chadwick, the "father" of scoring (and the man who gave us the eternal K for strikeout), observed: "It is about time that one system of

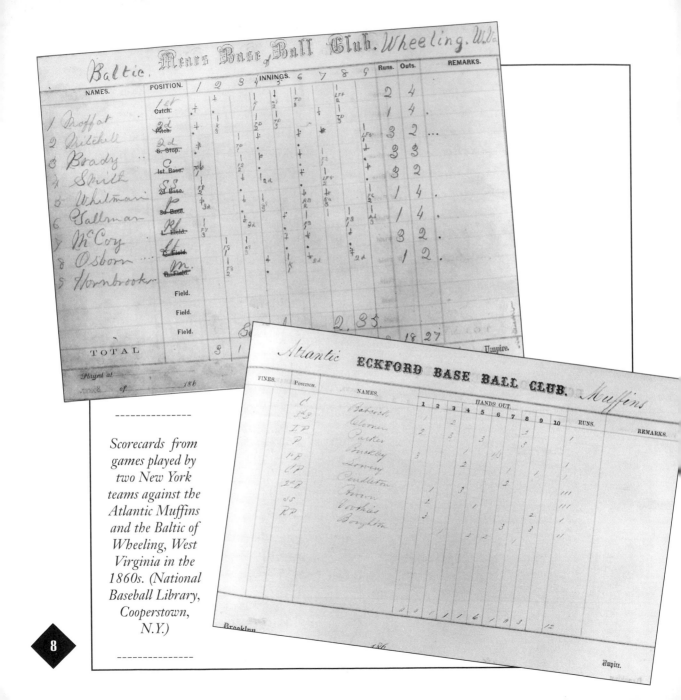

Scorecards from games played by two New York teams against the Atlantic Muffins and the Baltic of Wheeling, West Virginia in the 1860s. (National Baseball Library, Cooperstown, N.Y.)

scoring should be adapted throughout the country."

Then as now, there is no single system of scoring, and Chadwick's call for unity has gone unheeded. However, the urge to score and keep track of the game remains keen, for baseball begs to be recorded and recalled in shorthand.

Organized baseball has never made a secret of this fact. Listen to the words of the 1994 *New York Yankees Scorebook and Souvenir Program*: "Yankee fans can enjoy baseball more this summer by keeping score of the game." And the *Red Sox Official Scorebook Magazine* for 1994 talks of "rendering every game more enjoyable for baseball enthusiasts."

This is nothing new. A 1955 Washington Senators scorecard I own, from a game in which Ted Williams and Harmon Killebrew both played, informs us: "Half the fun at a ball game is keeping your own score," and for some time now the *Baltimore Orioles Program-Scorecard* has carried this caveat:

Warning! Be careful. Scoring a ball game can be habit forming. Proceed at your own risk!

Indeed, the fan who can sit there with a pen or pencil in hand and scorecard in his or her lap controls the information that gives every game texture and context. Announcer Warner Fusselle puts it simply: "If you really want to enjoy the game and understand it, you've got to score it."

Fusselle, who has scored and announced more than a thousand games, has developed a system for scoring that is so clear and detailed that he—or anyone with an eye for easy decryption—can read back every pitch, grounder, rain delay, and warning-track fly ball to left field. He did so for me in his office, grabbing the scorecard from Game 5 of the 1977 World Series and telling me *everything* that happened; he could have, given time, announced it pitch by pitch as if it were happening in front of his eyes. Writer Mike Lackey confirms Fusselle's rationale: "A great game, like the sixth game of the 1975 World Series, when Boston's Carlton Fisk beat Cincinnati 7–6 with a home run in the 12th inning, can still reach off the page years later with all of its original drama, building to a climax one batter at a time . . . Perhaps a chess player gets the same rush reading over play-by-play notation of a great game, but somehow it's difficult to imagine."

10

Lackey, by the way, has found added value in his scorecards. Writing in the Lima (Ohio) *News*, where he is an editor, he noted that in 1990 he started exchanging fifteen- to twenty-year-old score sheets with a fan in Massachusetts: "His style was different from mine, simpler and more ordered, all numbers and symbols; mine is expansive and eccentric, given to exclamation points and scribbled notes in the margins. But what struck me wasn't the differences. It was the realization that though we live 900 miles apart and have never met, the two of us could understand each other's score sheets as readily as we could have understood each other on the telephone. We were merely transcribing two different dialects of the same language."

One can also re-create games for others. Historian Doris Kearns Goodwin, appearing in Ken Burns's epic television series "Baseball," talked about her own obsession with scoring. It all started when her father encouraged her to score games from the radio while he was at work. He would come home when she was five or six years old and ask her to re-create the game by going through it an inning at a time. "And he never let me know that in the newspapers the next day he could have found out what had hap-

pened," she recalled. "I thought without me, he wouldn't know what had happened in the game. And so I was really like a little historian in those days and it was such a magic thing. When he would come home, I would sit on the porch with him, go over my meticulously kept game, and feel like I was saving it for him forever."

There are those who feel the primary value in keeping score is restricted to the period of the game itself. Ed Munson, who has been the official scorer for the California Angels since 1981, says that the fan who keeps score immediately gets "closer to the players and closer to the game." He adds, "Scorers properly feel that they are part of the game being played in front of them."

In his 1957 classic *How to Watch a Baseball Game*, Fred Schwed, Jr., points out that scoring allows you, among other things, to note toward game's end that the on-deck batter has struck out twice, once swinging. "Better yet," writes Schwed, "you can speak up and give this information to the people sitting near you, who will consider you a pretty profound character . . ."

Steve Fiffer in his book *How to Watch Baseball* argues for scoring as a means of getting the fan more deeply into the proceedings

----

*Public scoring. Large scoring
devices were once a staple of downtown America, where games in
progress could be watched. Here
fans watch a scoring machine in
front of the old Washington* Post
*building. (The Library of
Congress)*

by revealing hitherto unseen patterns, such as the number of men a particular pitcher retires on grounders rather than fly balls. He goes on to urge those who already score to do so in more detail.

"Start by recording whether the first pitch to each batter is a ball or strike," writes Fiffer. "Then, chart the success of the pitcher (and hitter) based on that pitch. Statistics indicate that the pitcher is significantly more successful if he gets his first pitch over for a strike."

Another possibility is recording the count on which each turn at bat is decided so that at the end of the game you can compare the pitcher's effectiveness when pitching ahead or behind in the count.

Fiffer adds that people who get hooked on scoring can move on to saving scorecards to look for even larger patterns—for instance, batters who tend to be at their best when their team is behind or tip-offs indicating when a certain pitcher is in trouble.

In some ways it is true that to see a person's completed scorecard is to see a personality revealed. In *Baseball by the Rules* authors Glen Waggoner, Kathleen Moloney, and Hugh Howard advise, "Next time you're at the ballpark, look over the shoulder of a few of the people keeping score. Chances are it will

be more revealing than a long look inside their medicine cabinets."

A bleacher fan in Wrigley Field, Michael Bojanowski of Cary, Illinois, has scored more than a thousand games over thirty years. "I have used scorekeeping to know the game as a participant would know it," he writes. "For one who has been a lifelong spectator, and never played real baseball, this is the best self-educational tool I know. Scoring is . . . an education in proper expectations: the way the game plays out, the way the action falls. Serious scorekeeping gives you a sense of context in which even a nonparticipant can know the true quality of the action he is seeing, removed from some of the emotional baggage of individual plays and at-bats. I think this is the greatest advantage that a 'scoring' fan possesses over one who doesn't."

Finally, there is the matter of historic linkage. There is no such thing as a "modern scorecard" in the same sense that there are MTV-generation "modern" scoreboards with names like Jumbotron and Diamond Vision. Nothing wrong with them, but they are one far, far cry from the hand-operated, drop-the-numbers-in-the-slot scoreboards of yore.

Scoring, on the other hand, which is as old as the American game, is still a low-technology proposition that operates on the same principles as the scoring systems and box scores pioneered by Henry Chadwick. Scoring has been getting rave reviews ever since. Writing about Chadwick's invention, Thomas S. Rice said in 1922, "If he was the inventor, that alone entitles him to a high position among the world's thinkers, for baseball scoring is the simplest, most easily learned, and most expressive of all the systems of shorthand ever invented."

The earliest-known scorebook is in the New York Public Library, and within it is the first scorecard for a game of baseball; the game was played on October 6, 1845. The first known newspaper box score showed up later that month.

Since, in baseball's early years, there were no major compilations of records as there are today, scoring became more and more important. An 1887 scorebook (*Cosgrave's Symbol Scorebook*) was sold as a personal record-keeping system "appreciated in cases of disputed plays and in the settlement of wagers made concerning differences of opinion as to games played in the past." In other words, there were times when the only place to look it up was on your own score sheet.

"The ability to keep track of every play is one of the beautiful things about baseball. The brief pause between batters gives you time to mark your scorecard without missing anything. It isn't that way in any other sport." So wrote C. C. Johnson Spink, editor and publisher of the *The Sporting News*, in a 1974 issue of the magazine.

Connie Mack wrapped in a warm blanket uses his scorecard to signal players during a cold April 10, 1937, exhibition city championship game between Mack's Athletics and the Phillies. The A's won 7-0. In his autobiography, My 66 Years in the Big Leagues, *Mack writes: "You have probably heard that I use my scorecard to convey information. Since our opponents know this, they keep a close watch on every movement I make with my scorecard, but this is fortified with many other devices." (National Baseball Library, Cooperstown, N.Y.)*

The scorecard has, in fact, been called the membership card into baseball. "No other American sport," writes Thomas Boswell of the Washington *Post*, "has anything that genuinely approximates the scorecard—that single piece of paper, simple enough for a child—that preserves the game both chronologically and in toto with almost no significant loss of detail."

The point is one that has fascinated a number of writers, including C. C. Johnson Spink, who wrote, "You can record every football play by means of a gridiron chart, but doing it requires concentration that interferes with your enjoyment of the game. And even then there's no simple way of recording the work of the offensive and defensive linemen unless they manage to get their hands on a ball some way or other . . . A basketball game can get away from you, because of the rapidity of the scoring, if you try to keep up with every field goal and free throw. And in hockey, you can note the goals and the assists and the penalties, but that's about all."

The membership-card notion seems to get stronger the further one goes back into one's youth. Writer Pat Edelson in *Outside Pitch* recalls his first scorecard, filled out when he was seven: "Writing their names in a scorecard made them real to me; recording their exploits made them heroes." He noted that his bond with the game was such that his first scorecards only listed first names because he didn't need a last name to know who was at bat.

"I've been thinking about that bond a lot lately, and wondering if keeping score may be one reason why so many people get hooked into baseball at a young age," Edelson writes. "Scoring, in some ways, is the perfect academic pursuit for a cerebral game, accessible to boys and girls, men and women."

Give the last word here to Connie Mack, who, at the end of a career spanning sixty-six years of big-league affiliation, put it this way: "Over the years I have found that keeping my own score has given much added interest to every baseball game I have watched—and I have lost count of the number."

How to Tend a Scorecard—The Basics

Scoring a ball game can be as simple or as complex as the fan wishes to make it. I've known fellow broadcasters who keep scorebooks as detailed as a researcher's calculations on atomic energy, and I've friends who content themselves with merely marking a large "O" on their score sheet when a batter is retired, a large "X" if he makes a hit, a "W" if he gets a base on balls, and an "E" if he reaches base on an error.

I doubt if there are any two people, fans, writers or broadcasters, who keep score with identical symbols and systems. I do know that any fan who acquires the habit of scoring his own ball games will find that it adds much to his enjoyment of the pastime.

—Red Barber,
Quoted in Joe DiMaggio's *Baseball for Everyone*

Scoring is based on a universal system of numbers and a varied collection of letters and symbols that allow for creativity and eccentricity: a common language with a rich and never-ending set of dialects that writer George Castle termed "a rudimentary, low-tech, yet striking record of the ebb and flow of a ballgame."

The basic system that is outlined in this chapter is quite universal, even as it offers some options and allows you to adopt and develop your own preferred variations. The

Standard blank scorecard © 1973, 1981. (Dave Loucks)

best systems, however, are the simplest. The next few lessons provide the basic information needed to score a game.

Lesson #1: THE GRID

The score sheet itself is a blank grid with the innings running across the top and spaces for the names of the players running down the left-hand side, with room for their position and, sometimes, uniform numbers. Usually there are extra lines for players who enter the game later, as there are extra columns for innings beyond nine. At the far right are columns to total each player's and team's results at the end of the game.

To score a game you need two grids, one for each team. One can buy books of score sheets, devise one's own sheet, or purchase the scorecard sold by vendors at the game.

Once you have all the players entered on your scorecard in batting order, you are ready to record each player's at bat, using the block in the scorecard corresponding to the particular batter and inning.

Some scorecards have blank blocks, some have blocks divided into four quarters, and others contain simple diamonds, sometimes preprinted with various symbols. One esti-

19

mate is that there are more than a hundred different scorecard designs on sale for baseball and softball use. If you're just starting out, don't worry about this diversity; stay with one simple style until you've gotten the hang of scoring. As you gain experience, you can add complexity.

Lesson #2: THE CODE

Although all systems are based on standard position numbers, there is variety in the scoring code. During the shortened 1994 baseball season, I collected a pile of official scorecards on visits to more than a half-dozen major league ballparks. All had informational sections on how to keep score, and all were markedly different. Something as simple as the symbol for a home run ranged from a straightforward HR (San Francisco Giants) to the rakish ⬦ (Baltimore Orioles). At the Astrodome, the home-run symbol looks like this □ and at Fenway Park it is this ≡ in the official scorecard; in the unofficial card sold outside the park a home run is a diagram of the base paths.

You need to know a basic list of abbreviations and letter symbols, all of which have to do with the disposition of the batter.

BB Base on Balls. Some people use W.
BK Balk
CS Caught Stealing
DP Double Play
DH Designated Hitter
E   Error, reached base on an
FC Fielder's Choice
FO Force-out
HB Hit Batsman (or, as some insist, Hit by Ball). Some people use HBP for Hit By Pitcher.
I   Interference
IW Intentional Walk. Some people prefer IBB.
K   Strikeout
PB Passed Ball
SB Stolen Base
SH Sacrifice Hit
SF Sacrifice Fly
WP Wild Pitch

In addition, you will need a code for hits. Perhaps the most common is one that uses a series of lines, no more complicated than these:

—   Single
=   Double

≡ Triple

≣ Home Run

Also common is this simple scheme:

1B Single

2B Double

3B Triple

4B or HR Home Run

Some team scorebooks, including those sold by the Houston Astros and the St. Paul Saints of the Northern League, suggest the use of this set of hieroglyphics:

— Single

⌐ Double

☐ Triple

☐ Home Run

The Baltimore Orioles suggest a set of lines that are, if nothing else, fun to draw:

╱ Single

╪ Double

╫ Triple

╫╫ Home Run

Finally, there are those who prefer the use of a diagram that describes the trip around the bases:

╱ Single

⟩ Double

◇ Triple

◇ Home Run

They all work; take your pick.

Lesson #3: BY THE NUMBERS

All scoring systems have a common numbering scheme for players in the field: pitcher, 1; catcher, 2; first baseman, 3; second baseman, 4; third baseman, 5; shortstop, 6; left fielder, 7; center fielder, 8; right fielder, 9.

Or:

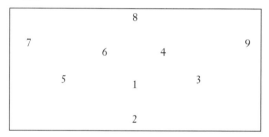

Another way to look at the defensive alignment is as a connect-the-dots diagram with this pattern, which some people find useful in visualizing the field numbers.

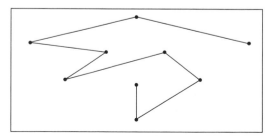

Memorize these positions well; every play in the field resulting in an out, except a strikeout, will require using them in the sequence the ball is touched. Assigning a putout is usually self-evident. Thus, if a batter is retired at first base on a grounder to third, you would note 5 - 3 on your scorecard; a fly ball to the center fielder would be simply noted as 8 since it was unassisted; a ground ball that caroms off the pitcher's glove and deflects to the second baseman, who then throws out the batter, would be scored 1 - 4 - 3. A strikeout is recorded K; the pitcher is awarded the strikeout, but the catcher gets credit for the putout. Other instances when the catcher is credited with the putout are if the batter is called out for being touched by his own batted ball or is called out for interfering with the catcher. According to baseball's rules, an assist is credited to "each fielder who throws or deflects a batted or thrown ball in such a way that a putout results, or would have resulted except for a subsequent error by any fielder."

A Digression on Numbers and Harry Wright's System

The number system makes a lot of sense. Since numbers refer to the position

and not to individuals, they are not affected by substitution: To find out who 8 or 5 was in a particular inning, one looks to the batting order. In Henry Chadwick's original system numbers were used, but they referred to the man's position in the batting order, which was confusing.

The modern system is not totally logical. Why is the shortstop numbered 6 instead of 5, which would be the logical sequence around the infield? The reason has been lost in history. Some suggest that the early shortstops were thought of as short outfielders rather than as members of the infield. This theory loses some credibility because the widespread use of 6 for the shortstop in scorecards bought in stadiums did not come into play until the 1920s. However, as early as 1890 the scoring system created by Harry Wright contained the modern numbering system, with 6 for the shortstop.

Wright's system, with an 1890 copyright and published as The Official Score Book *by A. J. Reach, Wright and Ditson, was much more like modern systems than Chadwick's creation, but with its own distinct feel. For instance, he used the symbol XX for a base made on a force-out. What made his system truly different, however, was that he noted if a base runner was left on base at the end of an inning by noting A, B, or C (for first, second, or third base, respectively) in the innings column opposite the base runner's name.*

If, however, the batter reaches base, the scoring block becomes a replica of the playing field. In scorecards with open blocks, home plate is in the lower left corner and progress around the bases is counterclockwise. A triple to center could be noted thusly:

If your score sheet has blocks with diamonds inside, the batter's progress follows the base paths, as this double to left suggests:

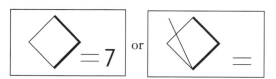

In the following example, the batter reached first on an error by the second baseman, stole second, went to third on a wild pitch, and scored on a passed ball. So runs can be seen at a glance, circle the notation in the lower left corner, or fill in the diamond, in the block of any batter who scores:

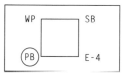

Or:

Lesson #4: FURTHER BASICS

At the end of each half inning, record a summary of runs and hits at the bottom of the column, so that a half inning with two runs and two hits looks like this:

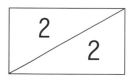

As the game progresses, you have a running total of each team's vital offensive statistics.

The best notation for a run batted in is a dot (•) recorded in the same place in each box so you can easily spot it. For two or more RBI, record two or more dots.

After the third out of each half inning, put a slash across the lower right corner of the last recorded block

so you are sure to start the next half inning one column over to the right.

Of course, one box begins to affect the next. Let's say our first batter, Robinson, walks, then steals second while the second batter, Smith, is batting. Smith bunts out 1–3 and Robinson advances to third. The third batter, Lopez, singles to right, scoring Robinson. Note that in this example there is a line from Smith's box to Robinson's for the sacrifice; experienced scorers will infer the connection, but if you are beginning, you may find the connecting line a useful tool to remember exactly what happened.

Robinson

Smith

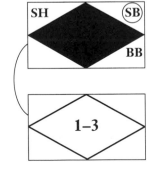

Lopez

On the right side of the inning-by-inning record, most scorecards contain blocks for each player's summary numbers: some combination of at bats (AB), runs (R), hits (H), doubles (2B), triples (3B), home runs (HR), walks (BB), strikeouts (SO), total bases (TB), stolen bases (SB), sacrifices (SAC), putouts (PO), assists (A), and errors (E). At the bottom of each club's page is usually space for recording each pitcher's game totals: innings pitched including fractions (IP), hits allowed (H), earned runs allowed (ER), walks (BB), and strikeouts (SO). Fractions of innings pitched are recorded in thirds, depending on the number of outs a pitcher has garnered in the last inning; for example 6 $\frac{1}{3}$ or 6.1. As the game progresses, official scorers use dots in the summary spaces to keep track of batters' and pitchers' key statistics to make it easier to tally them up at the end of the game.

ADVANCED SCORING TECHNIQUES

Any person claiming to be a baseball fan who does not also claim to have invented the quickest, simplest and complete method of keeping score probably is a fraud.

—THOMAS BOSWELL,
IN THE WASHINGTON *POST*

LESSON #5: AMPLIFICATIONS

Having mastered the basics, one can choose to go no further or to pick from a smorgasbord of amplifications to bring added dimension to the act of scoring . . . as in ⟨5L3⟩ if the 5-3 double play was the result of a line drive to third, or ⟨2F⟩ if the catcher caught the pop-up in foul territory.

A friend of mine uses a straight line over the traditional symbol to indicate a line drive, whether an out ⟨8̄⟩ or a hit ⟨1̄B⟩ ; a curved line over the symbol to indicate a pop fly ⟨8⟩ or ⟨1B⟩ ;or a straight line under the symbol to indicate a base-hit grounder ⟨1B̲⟩ .

Here are some other amplifications:

- The late Taylor Spink of *The Sporting News* advocated qualifying errors by the use of the small letter "t" to create the symbol ⟨Et⟩ in cases where the error is on a wild throw.
- Some scorers prefer to identify intentional walks by indicating IW or by underlining the usual walk symbol: <u>BB</u>.
- The *New York Yankees Scorebook/ Program* suggests the use of a wavy line ⟨∿⟩ in the appropriate block to indicate a substitute batter or pitcher.
- To more precisely track the progress of base runners, put a dot (•) on each base a runner stops on; for example: ⟨8•⟩

- Two small diagonal slashes on the bottom line of the block can indicate the last batter faced by the pitcher ⟨◇⟩, as can a solid line in the same place ⟨◇⟩. If a player is replaced, his/her last inning in the field can be noted ⟨◇⟩.

- In these contentious times, several scorers have developed a code for ejection from the game, with these as suggested possibilities: ⟨ej⟩ or just plain ⟨◇⟩.

- You may want to indicate the direction of a hit by placing the appropriate position number after the hit notation, so a double to left becomes ⟨=7⟩ or ⟨2B7⟩, or more diagrammatically: ⟨=⟩

- Writer Charles Einstein uses a little flag at the base of the letter F—like a sixteenth note in music—to indicate a foul fly as opposed to one in fair territory: ⟨F-7⟩ vs. ⟨F-7⟩.

- Another idea from Einstein is the use of the small letter "x" to indicate that an out is made on a runner on base ahead of the batter, when the batter reaches first base safely. Thus, if a man is on first and the batter forces him out at second, pitcher to shortstop, the batter's notation will be ⟨1-6x⟩. Alternately, the batter could receive ⟨FC⟩, for "reached first on fielder's choice," and the runner on first could be recorded out as ⟨0.1-6⟩.

Lesson #6: MARGINALIA

All scorers will encounter plays of such complexity that they defy distillation into the space on the scorecard. One posed by Bob Brown, a master scorer and author of the scoring system used by the Baltimore Orioles, is a play in which a batter is caught stealing second base after a pickoff and long rundown with a lot of fielders taking part—for example, a 1-3-4-3-6-3-4-2 play. In such cases one will want to find some place in the margin, record the play, and draw a line to the second-base corner or the player's box.

Notes in the margin also record details for which there is no symbol; for example:

- Rain delay: 1 hour, 12 minutes, top of 7th.
- Injured sliding
- Heavy wind blowing in at game time over 30 mph

- Game stopped to note batter's 1,000th major league RBI
- Stance like Mattingly (for a rookie who resembles Yankee star Don Mattingly at the plate)

If you are in doubt about how to note a play, write it out in longhand and figure it out later.

By all accounts, the hardest game to score is the major league All-Star Game, in which as many as four or five players may appear in the same slot in the lineup. It is even more of a challenge when, as it did in 1994 in Pittsburgh, the game goes into extra innings.

Lesson #7: USING COLOR AND DIAGRAMS

- *Color coding.* When David F. Riggs of Williamsburg, Virginia, heard that Joe Garagiola used color coding, he adopted Garagiola's system, which is to write walks in green (an automatic "go" from the pitcher), strikeouts in red (the ultimate "stop" by a pitcher), hits in blue, and all other plays in black.

Riggs then went one step further by putting the starting lineup in the domi-

nant color of the team in question. A Riggs scorecard shows the Texas Rangers lineup in blue and the Orioles lineup in orange. Player substitutes for both teams are written in black to quickly distinguish starters from their replacements.

Some years back, Art Cashion introduced a color code to the International Softball Congress tournament in which all official scorers use a red pen for hits and a black or blue one for everything else.

- *Diagrams.* Diagrammatic systems involve mapping the diamond as the runner makes his or her way around the bases, and are among the most appealing scoring variations. Hits are drawn, so that a single, double, triple, or home run looks like this: and or: and .

This system also allows you to use a directional line to indicate whether, say, a single is hit to right, left, or center. Another shows the influence of one batter on another, such as these two ways of showing a single and then an advance to third on a hit by the center fielder: or .

27

One of the advantages of diagrammatic systems is that trends are available at a glance. Robert Boynton of Del Mar, California, for instance, uses a solid dot for a ground out and a small circle for a fly out. Being able to see those ground outs enables him to look at a home-team scorecard and comment, "It is clear, for example, that when the Padres weren't striking out, they were beating the ball into the dirt."

Lesson #8: ASTERISKS, EXCLAMATION POINTS, AND OTHER SYMBOLS OF DEFENSIVE PROWESS!

"If you're scoring, do yourself a favor and put a star, a little asterisk, next to Segui's name," said veteran Baltimore Orioles broadcaster Chuck Thompson on June 30, 1991, as outfielder David Segui hit the wall catching a fly ball.

Thompson learned to score from the legendary Byrum Saam in 1947 and still uses that system, including the use of the asterisk (∗) for phenomenally good defensive plays.

Thompson is parsimonious about asterisks; he awards only a handful a year—for instance, giving Brady Anderson one for a

ball he lifts out of the laps of those in the bleachers. With a wistful look on his craggy face, Thompson admits that he does not award as many asterisks as he did "back in the days when Mark [Belanger] and Brooks [Robinson] wore the Orioles orange and black."

One is hardly restricted to the use of the asterisk. Baseball writer Charles Einstein has advocated the use of the exclamation point (!). Taking this one step further, D. J. Michael, in his "typewriter" method of scoring, wants to make sure that you put the number of the stellar player right next to the exclamation point: a great stop by the shortstop and peg to first for the out would be 6!-3. Still others, perhaps paying homage to the great Bill Veeck and his "exploding scoreboard" in Chicago, use little explosive puffs of smoke to punctuate a phenomenal moment.

Writer Thomas Boswell advocates circling in red the number of a player making a great defensive play. Warner Fusselle awards full circles for great plays and semicircles for half-great plays. On one of Fusselle's sheets, a play in which the first baseman digs the shortstop's throw out of the dirt would look like this: 6-3); but if it were truly spectacular it would be rendered 6- ③.

Fusselle uses other notations to distinguish one defensive play from another. The initials WT stand for balls caught on the warning track, and the word SUN denotes a ball caught despite the sun shining in the fielder's eyes.

"My own method has gotten much more complicated the longer I stay in this game," says Tim Wendell of *USA Today Baseball Weekly*. "In the old days, a fly ball was a simple 'F.' Now I've got 'F9' for a fly to right field; 'F89—r' for a great running catch in the center-field gap."

Wendell remembers when, as a cub reporter writing about the Giants for the San Francisco *Examiner*, he had a tough time finding the score on his cluttered card. "That was probably a result of me starring every semidecent play in the field," he recalls. "I was more impressionable then. Every fielder looked like a Gold Glover and

I gave them stars at every available opportunity. That is, until an old-time scribe glanced at my scorebook and announced that it looked more like the Milky Way than any ballgame he had witnessed in his thirty years."

CODA

Part of the charm of scoring is that it will not heel to conformity, despite the fact that there have been periodic calls for a uniform "national system." "Among baseball writers," says Leonard Koppett in *All About Baseball*, "no two scorebooks look identical in every detail, but by and large anyone can read anyone else's book for 90 percent of the plays recorded."

The fact remains, though, that your system is your own and there is no right or wrong way to score. You can pick and choose among the systems noted here, blending as you wish, or devise your own.

SCORING AND BASEBALL HISTORY FROM A TO Z

*H*aving mastered the basics of scoring, it's time to discover how scoring has influenced and enhanced the history of baseball.

What follows is an A-to-Z guide taking the reader through the whole realm of scoring, from the history of box scores to Presidential scoring habits; L. L. Bean's personal scoring system to concessionaire Harry M. Stevens's humble origins; records decided by scorers' judgments to Phil Rizzuto's famous "WW" notation. You can read it straight through or in pieces.

By the way, there are a few oddball-legitimate notions in here, including my personal reactions to two radical scoring notions—"team error" and an antonym for the error dubbed the "gem," or, as I like to call it, THE GEM.

A IS FOR ABBREVIATIONS AND SCORING SYMBOLS

Scoring became almost an obsession with me when I was a child, because my father taught me so proudly how to master all those miniature symbols.
—Doris Kearns Goodwin, speaking during Ken Burns's "Baseball"

Here is an expanded summary of scoring symbols and abbreviations that a scorer might encounter in his or her travels; it is especially useful in deciphering other people's good works. It includes several notations, such as EP, that are used only in softball.

A...(1) Assist. (2) Attendance at the game, as often appears in newspaper box scores.

AB...At Bat, or times a player has been At Bat. Used in box scores as well as scorecard team summaries.

AL...Active List, particularly referring to players who have come off the DL.

AVG...Average stands for *postgame* season's batting average in box scores.

BB...Base on Balls, although some people use W. Used to record a walk by a batter, but also used to record the number of walks given up by a pitcher in the pitcher's summary, or the number of walks earned by a team in a game summary and in box scores.

BI...Stands for total [runs] batted in during the game in most box scores; a.k.a. RBI.

BK / Bk...Balk.

BS...Blown Save opportunity.

BT / Bt...Bunt.

C...Center.

CG...Complete Game.

CS...Caught Stealing. Sometimes noted as OS for "out stealing."

D...Double.

DH...(1) Designated Hitter. (2) Less and less commonly, doubleheader.

DL...Disabled List.

DP...(1) Double Play. (2) In fast-pitch softball *only*, this is used for the designated player, an individual used on offense as one of nine hitters, like the DH in baseball, but who can also play defense. Contrast with EP, which is used only in *slow*-pitch softball.

E...Reached base on an Error. In scoring, ET or ETh can be used for an error in throwing, so that a throwing error by the third baseman would be ET-5.

EB...Extra Bases made on hits by a player while at bat, computed as one for a double, two for a triple, and three for a home run.

EIG...Extra-Inning Game.

EP...In slow-pitch softball *only*, this term stands for an optional extra player, used on offense only, who is the equivalent of the DH in baseball.

ER...Earned Runs Allowed; used to record the number of earned runs given up by a pitcher in the pitcher's summary. Remember that a run scored as a result of a fielding error is unearned.

ERA...Earned Run Average. In box scores, this is for *postgame* earned run average.

F...(1) Foul. (2) Fly. (3) Fly caught in fair territory to distinguish it from a flyout caught in foul territory, which some scorers indicate by

the use of the lowercase f or the symbol fF.

FC...Fielder's Choice.

fF/f...Foul fly (caught). This and the next are rarely seen today but appear in some older systems.

fFE...Foul fly (dropped).

fSF...Foul Sacrifice Fly.

FO...Force-out

FP...Fielding Percentage.

G...Game.

GA...Games Ahead.

GB...Games Behind.

GDP/GIDP...Grounded into Double Play.

GS...Games Started.

HB...Hit Batsman (or, as some insist, Hit by Ball).

HBP/HP...Hit by Pitch(er).

HR...Home Run.

I...Interference

IBB/IW...Intentional Walk.

IF...Infield Fly.

IP...(1) Innings Pitched. (2) In softball these initials are used to designate an illegal pitch.

K...Strikeout.

K/Kc...Out on a called third strike.

Ks...Out on a swinging third strike.

L...(1) Line Drive. (2) Left. (3) Number of games lost by a pitcher, as in W/L record.

LD...Line Drive.

LO/LOB...Runner(s) left on base.

LP...Losing Pitcher.

M...Muff of a fly ball. (Don't laugh. Many who learned to score in the 1950s from books like Arthur Mann's *How to Play Winning Baseball* used E for error on a ground ball and M for an error in the air. A6-M3 means that the shortstop gets an assist on the first baseman's muff of his throw.)

NP...Number of pitches thrown.

Obs...Obstruction.

OF...Outfield.

OS...(1) Out Stealing, an alternative to the more common CS for Caught Stealing. (2) Official Scorer.

PB...Passed Ball.

PH...Pinch Hit(ter).

PO...Putout.

PR...Pinch Runner.

R...(1) Right. (2) Runs Scored in a box score. (3) Runs Allowed in the pitcher's box-score summary.

RBI...In a box score it stands for the runs batted in thus far during the season.

RS...Runner(s) Stranded. This is a rarity, but there are a handful of scorers who use this when a batter leaves a base runner in scoring position.

S/SAC/Sac...Sacrifice.

SB...Stolen Base.

SF...Sacrifice Fly.

SH...Sacrifice Hit.

SHO...Shutout.

SO...Strikeouts. This notation is used only to record the number of strikeouts recorded by a pitcher in the pitcher's summary and strikeouts by a batter in the player's summary.

T...(1) Triple. (2) Length of time

to play the game.
TB...Total Bases recorded by a
    team in a game.
TP...Triple Play.
U...Unassisted Putout.
W...(1) Walk. (2) Wins,
    specifically the number of
    games won by a pitcher.
WP...(1) Wild Pitch. (2) Winning
    Pitcher.
WT...Notation used when a
    defensive player catches the
    ball on the Warning Track.
X...(1) Symbol used in the
    standings to indicate that a
    team has clinched its
    division title. (2) Something
    out of the ordinary (used
    rarely, as when a box-score
    compiler feels compelled to
    append a note to the summary
    of a game).

In addition to the number symbols used in baseball, there is this:

10...In slow-pitch softball *only,*
    there is an additional
    fielder who carries this
    designation. This player is

known as the short fielder or
rover.

B IS FOR BOX SCORES

----

*... "box scores." Only the
sophisticated will be able to
decipher them. The number of
people with the special knowledge to do this is limited, on
this continent, to a bare forty
or fifty million.*
—*Fred Schwed, Jr.,*
How to Watch a Baseball
Game, *1957*

A baseball game condensed, repackaged in black and white, or what Roger Angell once called "a precisely etched miniature of the sport itself," a box score has great allure. Writer Bill Conlin wrote, "The baseball box score is a pure American artform." Paul White of *USA Today Baseball Weekly* exulted, "Reading box scores makes me happy. The

34

longer I sit with my morning coffee and stare at them, the more I find that makes me smile."

To the uninitiated box scores are mysterious, but they will give themselves up to anyone willing to learn. "[They are] abbreviated history," wrote Fred Schwed, Jr., "two or three hours (the box score even gives that item to the minute) of complex activity, virtually inscribed on the head of a pin, yet no knowing reader suffers from eyestrain."

Box scores are a feature of newspaper sports sections, dating back to the nineteenth century. The "box" in the term alludes to the practice of placing the summary in a boxed-off part of the sports page. It has been said that the proliferation of out-of-town box scores set in agate in local newspapers was instrumental in making baseball grow as a true national game. They nourished the fan and drove the typesetters crazy.

Pioneer baseball writer Henry Chadwick has long been credited with creating the first box score, a fact that is noted on his plaque at the Hall of Fame in this unequivocal statement: "Inventor of the box score." For years the very first cited example was for a game played between the Gothams and the Knickerbockers that had begun on July 1, 1853, was postponed because of a storm, and was finished on July 5. A box score appeared in *Spirit of the Times* on July 9 with the initials F.W.T. and in the New York *Clipper* on July 16, 1853. This box score is hardly worthy of the name, as it counted only an individual's outs and runs.

However, an even earlier, and no less crude, box score from 1845 has come to light casting doubt on the idea that Chadwick invented the art form. There is no question, however, when it comes to the assertion that he developed it. Years ago, pioneer baseball writer Ernest J. Lanigan wrote that Chadwick "possibly did not invent the box score, but he improved it."

The use of the box score grew steadily, and by about 1876 almost every daily newspaper in the country was printing them.

Once hooked on a daily dose of box scores, it is hard to get away from them. I recall once recoiling in horror when I was told that one is not allowed to have a newspaper at Club Med resorts. There are some of us for whom the frustration over a baseball strike can be repressed all day and doesn't really hit home until we open the sports pages and find no box scores.

The box score is an American icon, fascinating children and adults, and with an influence beyond sports. In an essay, "Baseball in my Blood" (which appears in Ron Fimrite's fine anthology *Birth of a Fan*), Roy Blount, Jr., tells of making up imaginary box scores featuring his name along with several borrowed or imagined names. He tells of letting his pal Francis Rowe appear in one of those fantasy box scores, with Blount batting third and Rowe fourth. Blount went four for five that day ("The hardest thing," he admitted, "was keeping [my] batting average within the bounds of credibility"), while Rowe got only a couple of hits. "Francis gave me a funny look, whether because of the disparity in hits or because of finding himself statistically fictionalized. 'You hit more home runs than I do,' I said lamely."

In the same book, Robert Whiting has an engaging essay titled "A Fan Reborn" in which the pleasure of box scores surfaces again: "My enthusiasm for the Dodgers knew no bounds, even though I wasn't quite sure where Brooklyn was. I kept a daily diary of the team in a three-ring binder, logging with loving care box scores of every Dodger game, computing running totals of each Dodger's batting or pitching statistics, and noting important Dodger news as it occurred."

Perhaps the first person of note outside baseball to use the term "box score" was Franklin D. Roosevelt, who in the fall of 1936 began using the metaphor of the box score of government in relation to Congress's ability to pass New Deal legislation. Shortly thereafter the Republicans began to see, as one headline put it, "Errors in 'Box Score' of New Deal."

Since then, the ability of a president to get legislation passed has been regarded in terms of a box score. On August 12, 1948, President Harry S. Truman let Congress know he was upset that it had not acted on his eleven-point legislative program. The White House issued a statement summarizing the status of congressional action in the form of a "box score," and the headline in one paper read, "Truman 'Box Score' Hits Congress Again." Truman loved the notion of the box score and at one point in 1947 prepared one to show the state of U.S.–Soviet relations.

Among many later examples, one in particular comes to mind: the habit the wire services had of running "space box scores"—actual scoreboards—during the 1960s when the United States and the U.S.S.R. were locked in a lunar pennant race.

C IS FOR COLLECTING SCORECARDS— OBJECTS AND INFORMATION

----

*Next time you are leaving a ball park hang on to that scorecard. It will make an interesting souvenir tomorrow.
—John Sullivan*, Hobbies *magazine, 1957*

In 1957, when John Sullivan suggested that one might find it amusing to collect old scorecards and programs—not even implying that they might have any intrinsic value—he was probably regarded as eccentric. To suggest in 1957 that scorecards were a good investment would have been as silly as recommending the careful preservation of Mickey Mantle and Willie Mays baseball cards.

Fast-forward to the Sotheby's March 1991 sale that set the tone for the modern scorecard market. The 1933 *All-Star Score Book*, from Chicago, which originally cost a dime and features a drab ad for butter on its cover, fetched $3,300; a scorecard from the 1935 All-Star Game in Boston, which carried two ads on its cover and originally cost a nickel, brought $2,750; a dime program from the 1905 World Series earned $24,200.

It is interesting to note that scorecards that have actually been scored in are sometimes worth less than those that are unused, as baseball collector and broadcaster Ron Menchine points out. The exception would be something on the order of a scored program from Don Larsen's perfect game in the 1956 World Series. Menchine, along with Don Bevans, is the author of *Baseball Team Collectibles*, which lists hundreds of collectible programs, from $3 items up to the stratospheric examples sold at Sotheby's. Menchine adds that while the market for baseball cards has eroded some in recent years, the value of scorecards and programs has been slowly but steadily on the increase.

One of the things gleaned from looking at old scorecards is that there have been a lot of inferior systems at work. In fact, it would be hard to call some of them systems. The at bat boxes are often a quarter-inch long on each side and sometimes as small as an eighth of an inch. In many cases the scoring sheet in the scorecard is festooned with ads, leaving no room to tell how to score. On the

Scorecard,
Philadelphia vs.
New York, May 4,
1886. (Collection of
Ron Menchine)

STYLE IS EVERYTHING

BROOKLYN.

BATSMEN · POSITION		INNINGS.													SUMMARY.
		1	2	3	4	5	6	7	8	9	10.	11.	AB	R BH SH PO A E	
Collins,	2 B.														
Pinkney,	3 B.														
O'Brien,	C. F.														
Burns,	R. F.														
Foutz,	1 B.														
Terry,	L. F.														
Smith,	S. S.														
Lovett,	P.														
Bushong,	C.														
Total,															
Extra Player,															

2- BASE HITS 3- BASE HITS HOME RUNS STRUCK OUT UMPIRE

NEW YORK.

BATSMEN · POSITION		INNINGS.													SUMMARY.
		1	2	3	4	5	6	7	8	9	10.	11.	AB	R BH SH PO A E	
Tiernan,	C. F.														
Esterbrook,	1 B.														
Hornung,	S. S.														
Denny,	S. S.														
Burkett,	R. F.														
Clarke,	2 B.														
Buckley,															
Rusie,	P.	0	0	0	0	0	0	0	2						
Total,															
Extra Player,															

2- BASE HITS 3- BASE HITS HOME RUNS STRUCK OUT TIME OF GAME

16

Scorecard, Brooklyn Base Ball Club, 1890. Note the filled-in scorecard in what must have been the scorer's own system. (Collection of Ron Menchine)

Price 5 cents 25 or
Official Score Book
The
Brooklyn
Base Ball
Club Limited
Season of 1890.
WASHINGTON PARK,
5TH AVE. & 4TH ST.

39

Scorecard, Baltimore B.B. Club, 1896 (left), replete with advertisements. (Collection of Ron Menchine) Fan (right) doubling as a scorecard, 1907. (National Baseball Library, Cooperstown, N.Y.)

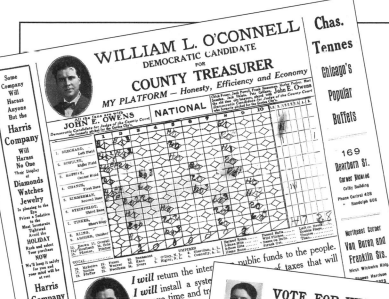
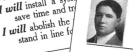

Advertisements for political candidates and for the revolutionary new "Curved Base Ball Bat," from the scorecard of the 1910 World Series in Chicago. (Collection of Ron Menchine)

CHAMPIONS 1912

RED SOX

Giants - 2
Red Sox - 3
8th Game - Oct 15, 1912

WORLD'S SERIES

FENWAY PARK · BOSTON ·

Souvenir Biography and Score Book ·

Price, 10 Cents

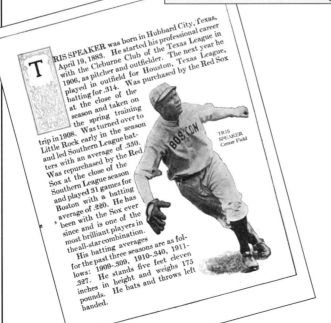

TRIS SPEAKER was born in Hubbard City, Texas, April 19, 1883. He started his professional career with the Cleburne Club of the Texas League in 1906, as pitcher and outfielder. The next year he played in outfield for Houston, Texas League, batting for .314. Was purchased by the Red Sox at the close of the season and taken on the spring training trip in 1908. Was turned over to Little Rock early in the season and led Southern League batters with an average of .350. Was repurchased by the Red Sox at the close of the Southern League season and played 31 games for Boston with a batting average of .220. He has been with the Sox ever since and is one of the most brilliant players in the all-star combination.

His batting averages for the past three seasons are as follows: 1909-.309, 1910-.340, 1911-.327. He stands five feet eleven inches in height and weighs 175 pounds. He bats and throws left handed.

TRIS SPEAKER
Center Field

Scorecard, 1912 World Series, Giants vs. Red Sox, Fenway Park. The program contained elegant biographies, such as the one of Tris Speaker shown here. (Collection of Ron Menchine)

A variety of score-cards: clockwise left to right, Chicago, Federal League, 1914; St. Louis Browns, 1953; World Series, Shibe Park, Philadelphia, 1914. (Collection of Ron Menchine)

plus side, the ads are often nostalgic reminders of simpler—and less expensive—times. A 1941 scorecard sold for a nickel at Griffith Stadium in Washington offers Washington Redskins season tickets (including lower box seats) for $9.90 including tax. One finds ads for everything from long-gone snacks (Elmer's Chee-Wees, a delicious cheese snack) to five-cent cigars. Indeed, it's fair to say that historic scorecards are Americana of the highest order.

D IS FOR DETAILS, DETAILS, AND MORE DETAILS

A baseball fan has the digestive apparatus of a billy goat. He can—and does—devour any set of diamond statistics with insatiable appetite and then nuzzle hungrily for more.
—*Sportswriter Arthur Daley*

Baseball numbers are being processed by highly advanced scoring methods. In 1984, a group called Project Scoresheet created a copyrighted "state-of-the-art" scoring system replete with more than two hundred scoring codes of such precision that there were close to one hundred for where a batted ball landed, including fifteen coded landing zones in foul territory and no fewer than thirty-five outfield locations.

An inside-the-park home run lined into deep center field, for example, would be noted as HR8/L8XD, while the line SB2(2-3(E2/TH)) lets one in on the details of a stolen base with the catcher making a throwing error (E2/TH) to second base that allows the runner to move to third base (2-3). There is a provision for scoring each pitch, including letter codes for missed bunt (M) and foul ball on a pitchout (R).

There is even a separate code, NDP, for the rare play in which two outs are recorded but it is not considered a double play.

The intent was to record everything in proper context and with full description so that someone could later determine exactly where a ground ball hit to the outfield went through the infield. The daunting factor for the average scorer is that it is so hard to decipher, let alone record. For instance, the letter P, depending on its context on the sheet, can stand for pinchrunner, pitchout, or pop-up. The number 2 can represent the catcher, a throw to second, or a runner on second.

Project Scoresheet, as one participant put it, "collapsed of its own weight" in 1990. It sired two offspring: STATS Inc., which was the first widely known system to record each pitch and the direction, distance, and velocity of each ball hit into play; and a nonprofit group operating under the name of The Baseball Workshop. The STATS database has been used to create *The Bill James/ STATS Major League Handbook* and *The STATS Baseball Scoreboard*. (STATS can be reached at STATS, Inc., 7366 N. Lincoln Ave., Lincolnwood, IL 60646-1708.)

While scoring at this level is a reality, it will probably never appeal to more than the few hundred devout souls who contribute their research to these systems.

For most of us, it's a comfort to know it's all there. The number of games compiled by both groups up to the time of the August 1994 strike was 22,806, with more than 1.72 million plays. This does not include the work of an organization known as Retrosheet, which is attempting to come up with detailed records of games played between 1871 and 1983 (Scoresheet's work began at the begin-

ning of the 1984 season) and whose good works will be discussed shortly.

E IS FOR THE EISENHOWER-COOLIDGE CONTINUUM

When I was a small boy in Kansas, a friend of mine and I went fishing and as we sat there in the warmth of the summer afternoon on a river bank, we talked about what we wanted to do when we grew up. I told him that I wanted to be a major league baseball player, a genuine professional like Honus Wagner. My friend said that he'd like to be president of the United States. Neither of us got our wish.
—*Dwight D. Eisenhower, quoted in* Sports Illustrated

Evidence suggests that President Dwight D. Eisenhower was the most celebrated scorer among great public figures.

President Dwight
D. Eisenhower
scoring a
Washington
Senators opener
with House
Republican leader
Joe Martin (to his
right), looking at
his scorecard, and
Senators' owner
Calvin Griffith
(left). (The Library
of Congress)

When he returned from Europe and the Great Allied Victory he attended a ball game at the Polo Grounds in New York and eagerly began scoring. He was interrupted so many times by a parade of local politicians eager to shake the hero's hand that he had to abandon his scorecard. As President he loved to score in ink and was commonly photographed scoring in the presidential box at Griffith Stadium.

Eisenhower is one of two known scorecard-carriers to have lived in the White House. First Lady Grace Coolidge was known to keep a "perfect scorecard" and to stay in the presidential box at Griffith Stadium long after the President had slipped away. She had learned to score in college and saw it as an integral part of enjoying a ballgame. She went to as many games as she could, visited the players in the dugout, and held on to her scorecards.

President Cal didn't see the point. In fact, he was so indifferent that at the opening game of the 1924 World Series, he rose to leave when the score was tied at the end of the ninth inning. Grace Coolidge had to literally pull him back into his seat by his coattails.

First Lady Grace Coolidge, a determined scorekeeper, depicted with President Coolidge, reproduced from a Washington Senators program. (The Library of Congress)

The Eisenhower-Coolidge pairing is interesting because it emphasizes a point that scorers have long observed: women are as likely to score as men. Another prime example was Jean Yawkey, majority owner of the Boston Red Sox from 1976 until her death in 1992, at which time this line appeared in her obituary in *USA Today Baseball Weekly*: "Through last season, Mrs. Yawkey was a figure at Fenway Park sitting in her rooftop box with her trademark binoculars and scorecard."

Back during the summer of 1959, the people of San Francisco were enjoying the nov-

elty of having their first major league team. The former New York Giants were playing in Seals Stadium. Bucky Walter of the San Francisco *News Call-Bulletin* took a look at scoring in the Bay Area and came up with two conclusions. The first was predictable:

(1) "Each play at Seals Stadium is traced on thousands of scorecards in a helter-skelter of symbols, basically alike but with as many modifications as human ingenuity can contrive."

(2) Many of these scorers were women, or as Walter put it in the arcane language of the time: "Milady is as enthusiastic about

scoring as the man of the house, we learned after snooping the downtown district."

Fact is, women have been keeping score in large numbers for decades.

There have even been several female official scorers. Elisa Green Williams was one. During the 1890s she scored for the Chicago White Stockings. Ms. Williams was a friend of the team's owner, Albert Goodwill Spalding.

The reaction? There was none because in those days the practice was to keep the name of the scorer a secret to protect him or her from the ire of dissenting players and fans. Ms. Williams would sit with one of the players' wives on either side of her while she secretly scored each game.

F IS FOR SCOREKEEPING IN FRENCH

Whene'er I hear French spoken
as I approve
I find myself quietly falling in love.
—*E. R. Bulwer-Lytton*, Lucile,
1860

COMMENT MARQUER UNE FEUILLE DE POINTAGE

From a 1968 Montreal Expos scorecard:

Il existe une méthode très simple d'indiquer sur votre feuille de pointage tout ce qui se passe au cours d'une partie de baseball.

Chaque joueur sur le losange a un numéro: lanceur—1; receveur—2; premier-but—3; deuxième-but—4; troisième-but—5; arrêt-court—6; champ gauche—7; champ centre—8; champ droit—9.

On emploie des symboles pour indiquer de quelle façon le joueur a atteint le but ou a été retiré.

— (Single) un simple
⌐ (Double) un deux-buts
⌐ (Triple) un trois-buts
☐ (Home Run) un circuit
E (Error) erreur
FC (Fielder's Choice) choix de l'intérieur
HP (Hit by Pitcher) atteint d'un lancer
WP (Wild Pitch) mauvais lancer
SB (Stolen Base) but volé
SH (Sacrifice Hit) coup sacrifice
PB (Passed Ball) balle passée
BK (Balk) balk

K (Strikeout) retrait au bâton
BB (Base on Balls) buts sur
    balles
FO (Force-out) jeu forcé
SF (Sacrifice Fly) ballon
    sacrifice

Le coin inférieur gauche du carré doit être considéré comme le marbre. Le coin inférieur droit est le premier coussin. Le coin supérieur droit le deuxième but et le coin supérieur gauche le troisième but.

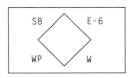

Pour mieux vous faire comprendre, voici un exemple: le frappeur se rend au premier coussin sur un but sur balles (W) il passe au deuxième sur une erreur du joueur d'arrêt-court (E-6); il vole le troisième but (SB) et croise le marbre sur un mauvais lancer (WP).

Tout retrait au champ intérieur ou extérieur doit être indiqué sur la feuille de pointage. Ainsi, vous marquez 6-3 si le frappeur cogne un roulant à l'arrêt-court qui relaie au premier-but. Pour un ballon au champ gauche, le symbole est F7. Dans le cas d'une balle fausse attrapée au champ droit vous inscrivez 9F. Pour un double-jeu, de l'arrêt-court au deuxième-but, au premier-but, vous indiquez 6-4 et 4-3 dans le carré des joueurs en question.

G IS FOR GEMS AND ERRORS

Batters are rewarded for their exploits. The hit that puts them on base, be it ever so humble and scratchy, is chalked up in the record book. It fattens batting averages and is tallied in baseball annuals. But what about the unsung and unchronicled defensive plays—the leaping and shoestring sparklers that steal hits and save games?
—Mel Allen, 1954

Since its inception baseball has had a demerit system charging players with errors. Men who have been dead for several generations are still listed in baseball reference books for the errors they made while dreaming of Clara Bow, Theda Bara, or other sirens of the silent screen. Errors are eternal. Errors are everlasting. Some monumental errors even have special names affixed to them and the men who made them, like Fred Snodgrass of the Snodgrass Muff, and Fred Merkle of the infamous Merkle's Boner that cost the New York Giants the 1908 National League Championship. Poor Bill Buckner will forever be remembered for the ball that went through his legs in the sixth game of the 1986 World Series.

In July 1954, Mel Allen, after announcing no fewer than 3,000 major league games, wrote an article for *This Week* magazine in which he advocated a "Bill of Rights" for fielders in which there would be a box-score credit for a "sparkling play," which he termed "gem." It would be the healthy antidote to the 2,500 errors that Allen said would be recorded during the '54 season.

From the perspective of 1954, Allen reeled off a group of actual plays that deserved special recognition. The first that came to him was Al Gionfriddo's "miraculous leaping stab of Joe DiMaggio's 415-foot bid for a homer at the bullpen gate in a 1947 World Series game which the Dodgers won thanks largely to Al's grab."

Allen recalled many others, including a sin-gle-handed double play by Yankee Yogi Berra in which he scurried in front of the plate, picked up a squeeze bunt, tagged the batter out, and whirled around to tag a man out at the plate. Then there was the time Lou Boudreau of the Indians dashed over from the shortstop position to scoop up a hot grounder behind third base and, while falling down, underhanded the ball to the third baseman, who threw the batter out at first. You could add your own gems: Dwight Evans's catch of Joe Morgan's shot to right in the sixth game of the 1975 World Series; any number of Ozzie Smith's wizardlike moments; or a memorable play in your softball league playoffs.

Back in 1954, a lot of people sided with Allen—"It would mean a new scoring system, but it's worth the trouble," opined Lou Boudreau—but the idea went nowhere . . . well, *almost* nowhere.

I was in ninth grade at Nathaniel Hawthorne Junior High School in Yonkers, New York, when I first read Allen's "Something New in Baseball" in July 1954. I swallowed it whole, and had mentally awarded fourteen gems by the end of the summer. Along the way I have forgotten the list, but I do recall it beginning, alphabetically, with Avila, Bobby.

A gem looks like this (◆), or G!

Award them sparingly.

Gem! Brooks Robinson demonstrates why many scorers have found a way to note defensive excellence. (Baltimore Orioles)

H IS FOR HINDSIGHT

I remember one game I got five hits and stole five bases, but none of it was written down because they forgot to bring the scorebook to the game that day.
—Negro League Star James "Cool Papa" Bell on the "record books"

Suppose somebody told you that you had to go back in time and record every out and every hit in baseball from the beginning. Suppose you could have help, but only from unpaid volunteers. Suppose you were David Smith, a programmer, sabermetrician, and college professor.

A few years ago, Smith set out to collect the records of the tens of thousands of games played between 1871 and 1983 (when the aforementioned Project Scoresheet kicked in) and to enter them, a play at a time, into a database.

In 1994 Smith's project, which he calls Retrosheet, became a nonprofit corporation whose goal is to digest every at bat in the history of the game. Gathering records from teams and other sources, Smith and a network of volunteers had, as of this writing, entered between 8,000 and 9,000 games into the computer, with 150,000 or so games to go.

Why? "Pure and simply," says Smith, "this is being done to complete the historic record. To build a total record that people can use as they see fit."

One of the prime uses will be for analysis of trends and effects. "For instance, we are creating the means by which we will be able to determine the effect of the rise of relief pitching on batting," Smith explains.

Some people are starting to use these records for computer simulations and games, and others come to Retrosheet for personal reasons. Says Smith: "I already get three or four requests a year from people who want to get the scoring of the first game they ever saw but may only know that it was in 1969, that so-and-so had pitched and so-and-so had tripled late in the game."

Those who get involved are likely to find all sorts of oddities. For instance, on July 18, 1964, in the second game of a doubleheader the Cubs scored five runs against the Dodgers in the second inning. The Cubs had

nine batters that inning and saw a total of ten Dodger pitches—there was only one swinging strike.

In order to volunteer or get more information on this project, write to:

David W. Smith
Retrosheet
6 Penncross Circle
Newark, DE 19702

I IS FOR I SCORE, THEREFORE I AM—THE SCORER'S CREED

Everybody knows that the manner of keeping score, like religion, is a personal matter. —*Lindsey Nelson, from his book* Hello Everybody, I'm Lindsey Nelson

----

Is there a belief system at work here? Something between dogma and conventional scorer's wisdom? Certainly. Here is an attempt to codify it.

I. That, in the words of the late Red Smith, "every game is a new game, different from any other that's ever been played" and that it is my privilege to record this unique event in a simple, written language that encompasses the infinite variety of baseball.

II. That the act of scoring makes the man, woman, or child in the stands part of the game.

III. That there is no such thing as a right or wrong system of scoring; but all that is required of a good system is that the scorer be able to call it back—as if announcing the game on radio—days, months, or years later and that, no matter how expansive or eccentric, another scorer will be able to read it in a matter of moments.

IV. That, despite a small but growing group that believes scoring is a job for laptop computers and all numbers belong in databases, you shouldn't be intimidated by the twentieth century. All the broadcasters working in the majors in 1994 and all the official scorers at work in the majors still process numbers and letters with nothing more sophisticated than a #2 pencil. Besides, you can use a #2 pencil to spread mustard.

V. That scoring is the same basic act at every level of baseball and softball, but that the lower one goes on the ladder, the higher the stakes—that is, few care how you score a play from the bleachers in the majors, but this is certainly not the case when the players on the field are under fifteen years of age.

VI. That the old umpire's dictum works for scorers as well, to wit: "Keep your eye on the baseball because nothing can happen without it." If you look away from the ball when what is about to happen looks obvious, you will miss the extraordinary—say, a delayed steal, a pickoff, or watching a foul ball turned into a triple by the winds at play inside Candlestick Park.

VII. That scorers react and never anticipate. As superscorer Warner Fusselle puts it, "Never add a pinch hitter or a relief pitcher until they are actually in the game. Otherwise you'll spend all your time erasing."

J IS FOR JUDGMENT CALLS

You may not always agree with the scorekeeper's decision, but you must follow the decision and record it on your scorecard.
—Traditional advice to fans keeping scorecards

Purists insist that the man or woman in the stands has some sort of social contract to follow the rulings of the official scorer in matters of scoring. But some otherwise law-abiding types will leave the ballpark with head held high clutching a *deviant* scorecard, having scored plays as they saw them.

Nelson Eddy, a Nashville public relations executive and devout scorer, defends his own judgment: "You think it was an error and the official scorer calls it a hit, you can record it as an error. You control your own scorecard. It is the game that you saw with your own two eyes, not the one in the paper the next morning."

Perhaps surprisingly, at least one official scorer agrees with Eddy. "The fan in the stands has every right to see a play differently and record it as such," says Ed Munson, official scorer for the California Angels, "but if it were me, I'd note that my call differed from the official one."

This individualistic approach is not restricted to fans. Sportswriters have been known to deviate from the official line. Legendary writer H. G. Salsinger of the Detroit *News* kept his own score, and from time to time his scoring would differ from the record sent to the league headquarters.

Bob Addie, in his book *Sportswriter*, recalls Salsinger reacting to a play that the official scorer called a hit. "Not in my paper," Salsinger roared. "It's an error." In the next day's *News*, the play was an error.

K IS FOR K AS IN STRIKEOUT

Once again, he winds up and goes for the K.
—Traditional line of sportscaster describing a pitcher racking up strikeouts

----

K. It is the most abiding of abbreviations, taken, by all accounts, from the back rather than the front of the word "strike."

It was the invention of Henry Chadwick, notwithstanding an article in *The Sporting News* of June 12, 1965, asserting that the first person to use the K was M. J. Kelly, a baseball writer for the New York *Herald* and editor of the *DeWitt Guide for 1868*. True, Kelly used it, but he had learned it from Chadwick, who, among other things, became the *Herald's* first baseball editor in 1864, and who used the K symbol in 1868 in *Beadle's Guide*, of which he was the editor. From time to time, it has been further asserted that the K was Kelly's appropriation of his own initial, but this is unsubstantiated speculation—similar to the occasionally mentioned notion that K is the letter that most resembles a batter standing at the plate.

On a number of occasions Chadwick told how the scoring system was created in the early 1860s. One of the most complete renditions appeared in 1883 in *Peck and Snyder's Scorebook*, which was created by Chadwick. "Over twenty years ago we prepared a system of short-hand for the movements of contestants in a baseball match, which system is now familiar to every scorer in the country. The abbreviations of this system were prepared on the mnemonics plan of connecting the abbreviated words in some way or another with the movement to be described . . . "

So it was that Chadwick was able to explain: "K stands for 'struck out' as it was the prominent letter of the word strike, as far as remembering the word was concerned." At another point in the discussion of his system, Chadwick notes that "the letter K in struck is easier to re-member in connection with the word, than S."

Most of Chadwick's ideas have long ago been dropped, including the use of L for fouL, which is totally consistent with the use of K. Incidentally, Chadwick's system was unlike any that have come into use in the twentieth century. For one thing, it used letters, not numbers, for defensive plays: for instance, C for a putout at third and RO for a putout between bases. There were six error symbols, including ● for a muffed ball and 0 for a dropped fly ball.

L IS FOR L. L. BEAN'S SYSTEM, THE E.Z. RADIO BASEBALL SCORE CARD, AND OTHER ATTEMPTS AT THE GREAT AMERICAN SCORECARD

In order to enjoy a better baseball game, keep a more accurate record for future reference, and stimulate enthusiasm in the new fans, especially the ladies and children, to learn how to keep score, I have created this simplified easy system of keeping score...

L. L. BEAN'S

35¢

Simplified Baseball

Score Book

Especially Adapted
for
Night Scoring

L. L. Bean
Originator and Author
Freeport, Maine

L.L. Bean's Simplified Baseball Score Book and a sample (right) of the system for scoring the Brooklyn Dodgers' loss to the New York Yankees in the second game of the 1953 World Series. (Author's collection)

AT _N.Y._ DATE _Oct. 1, 1953 – 2d Game W.S._

TEAM _Dodgers_ SCORER _L L Bean_

POS.	PLAYER	AVE.	1	2	3	4	5	6	7	8	9	HITS
2d	Gilliam	289										o
s	Reese	271	3/					W		W		2
c	Snider	336										o
l	Robinson	329										1
C	Campanella	312										o
1st	Hodges	302		W						①		2
r	Furillo	344						2				2
3d	Cox	291		W		1						1
P	Roe	11/3		①								1
TOTALS HITS			9	1	0	0	3	2	1	0	1	1
RUNS			2	0	0	0	2	0	0	0	0	

HOME RUNS _0_ 3 BASE HITS _1_ 2 BASE HITS _2_ E _0_ W _4_ S.O. _3_

Key to 2nd Game World Series 1953 (Dodgers)

Gilliam — Grounded to S. S. Flied to center. Flied to 2nd. Grounded to S. S. Flied out to Center field.

Reese — 3-base hit to right. Flied to right. Hit to center. Walked. Walked.

Snider — Popped out to Catcher. Flied out to center. Struck out. Grounded to 2nd. Grounded out to 2nd base.

Robinson — Flied to center. Flied to left. Hit to left. Popped out to 1st base.

Furillo — Grounded out to 3rd. Hit to right. 2-Base Hit to right. Flied out to right.

Cox — Walked. 2-Base hit to left. Grounded out to 3rd. Grounded to S. S.

Roe — Grounded out to Pitcher. Struck out. Struck out. Hit to left.

—Introduction to Anthony Johncola's 1949 scorekeeping system on file in the National Baseball Library in Cooperstown. Like other "simplified" systems it is fairly complicated, with no fewer than thirty-four batting and fielding columns (seventeen for each team) to tally at the end of the game.

On October 2, 1941, James M. Berry of Detroit, the owner of the Berry Rug and Furniture Company, wrote to President Franklin D. Roosevelt. Berry was upset that FDR was so busy with affairs of state that he could not take time to throw out the first ball of the World Series. He was, however, encouraged by the fact that the White House had announced that the chief executive would listen to the fall classic on the radio.

Berry then wrote: "Next to seeing the game itself and to get a little relaxation for you I am enclosing some blanks of a new simple understandable baseball score card that virtually puts the radio listener in the grandstand behind home plate."

The letter enclosed a pile of scorecards called Berry's E-Z Radio Baseball Score Cards.

Fact #1: This may have been the most complicated system ever devised, with a totally new set of notations and marks that turned a double play into something akin to a marginal Robert Motherwell painting.

Fact #2: It was as much an advertisement for Berry's store as it was a system. "Visualize the whole panorama of the game as it progresses," read the come-on at the top of the card. "See the tense situations, runners on base when a hit may mean winning the game. Enjoy the values at Berry's."

Folks are forever trying to revolutionize the act of scoring—with the result that the system is usually (a) more complicated, (b) confusing, (c) lacking some key information, or (d) all of the above.

An example or two should suffice. A system in use for a professional game played at Buffalo in 1877 yielded infinite detail on individual acts such as fielding assists, but gave no information on the sequence of events. Looking at the scorecard, one has no sense of when and how runs are scored. To make matters even more confusing, the player positions are designated by letters—the third baseman, for example, is D.

A system copyrighted in 1887 (*Cosgrave's Symbol Scorebook*) was fairly routine but seemed pitched to resolving arguments and, oddly, wagering on games already played. The value of the system "will be at once appreciated in cases of disputed plays and in the settlement of wagers made concerning differences of opinion as to games played in the past."

In 1954, no less a figure than L. L. Bean of Freeport, Maine, came out with his own system, which was a reaction to the fact that more and more games were being played at night. The cover of L. L. Bean's Simplified Baseball Score Book ($.35) announces in large letters, "Especially Adapted for Night Scoring."

Bean's system stressed simplicity. He based it on five easy-to-read symbols—W for walk, E for error, fc for fielder's choice, a circle for an out, and a line with a dot on the end for a hit ↗. One play would be distinguished from another by arrows, dots, and numbers. For instance, a triple to left would look like this ↖3, a fly ball to right field like this ○̇, and a double play like this ⒟, with D being Bean's code for double play.

In typical Bean fashion the system is pragmatic and clearcut, but it never caught on. Perhaps it was too simple and therefore imprecise. Bean's ⒟ was no substitute for knowing that a double play was of the 6-4-3 or the 1-3-4 vari-

ety. The system was so simple that he chose not to identify defensive players at all.

A used copy of one of Bean's score books recently has come into the author's possession. The young man, named Robert, who took the book with him to score games in Boston and New York and to record the exploits of men named Yastrzemski, Maris, and Mantle tried the Bean system but soon drifted back to the traditional world of K's and 5-4-3 plays.

L. L. Bean never revolutionized scoring—he had to settle for revolutionizing catalog retailing.

M IS FOR THE METAPHOR OF SCORING . . . WITH A LENGTHY DIGRESSION ON SCORECARDS, HOT DOGS, AND PEANUTS

Q: What's a Metaphor?
A: To play baseball on.
—The author's favorite baseball pun after the one about baseball in the Bible ("In the Big Inning")

Born in London but living in Niles, Ohio, before the turn of the century, Harry M. Stevens was an iron puddler who was out of work because of a strike. With no money coming in, he took to the streets and began selling copies of a little book titled *Irish Orators and Oratory*.

One summer afternoon in 1887 he decided to take the afternoon off and went to the old Columbus ballpark to see some baseball. It struck him that the scorecard sold to patrons was a sorry little thing in need of improvement. Stevens reasoned that a better-looking and more informative scorecard could be produced, with the increased printing costs and a small profit for himself coming from advertising. He got the scorecard concession for a fee of $700. His idea worked in Columbus, where Stevens created a selling call that will forever be associated with the game: "Get your scorecard! You can't tell the players without a scorecard."

From this start in Columbus he obtained the scorecard concession at the Polo Grounds in New York in 1894 and moved on to create a national empire at ballparks, racetracks, and other sporting venues, where he sold food—peanuts, popcorn, CrackerJacks, and especially hot dogs.

Stevens carried the sobriquet of the man who parlayed a bag of peanuts into a million. Writer Red Patterson of the old New York *Herald Tribune* memorialized him a few years after his death: "To him must go the credit for that great institution the hot dog, and also for the popularity of its brother, the double-jointed peanut." Stevens didn't invent either, but he is mainly responsible for their high place on the list of American gastronomic pleasures.

The selling of the first ballpark hot dog was a spontaneous move. The fact was that Stevens kept some wieners in his Polo Grounds kitchen for his pals and for the press, but he had never thought of selling them to fans. One cold, drizzly, fateful day, Stevens realized that he was not going to sell much ice cream or cold soda pop. It dawned on him to sell hot frankfurters. He dispatched one vendor to buy a thousand wieners, another to obtain a thousand rolls, and a third to bring back three quarts of mustard and pickle relish.

The fans loved it, and before long the snacks were being called hot dog sandwiches. Later the term was used to describe a player given to theatrics and showing off, giving rise to the pure speculation that this was because

NEW YORK	1	2	3	4	5	6	7	8	9	10	AB	R	1B	PO	A	E
McCormick Bresnahan c f	F-7			F-7				5-4 3b			4	0	0	1	1	1
Browne r f	1-3		F-9			9-4 5 H	P8 F2				4	0	1	0	1	
Devlin Dunn 3 b	z		5-43 1 H		F-9		F-3				3	1	1	2	1	0
McGann 1 b	6-3		F-3		4-5 2	F-9					3	0	0	13	0	0
Mertes l f		3-4 2	B-3					4-3			3	0	0	2	0	0
Dahlen s s		1-5	1+1 H		FC	5-4 H	8b 5 2				3	1	2	1	4	1
Gilbert 2 b		4-3		F-1		9-5 FC		H			4	0	1	4	4	0
Warner or C			6-3			z	F-7	F-8			3	0	0	3	0	0
or McGinity P			7-55 5 H	F-9				H	L-3		3	0	2	6	1	1
											1	0	0	0	0	0
TOTAL	0	0	1	2	0	6	0	0	1		31	2	7	27	18	4

CHICAGO	1	2	3	4	5	6	7	8	9	10	AB	R	1B	PO	A	E
Slagle l f	3-52 V-6	F-6		5B 2 H		F-9					4	1	1	3	0	0
Casey 3 b	2-3 5H	4-3		9C			F-8				3	0	0	2	2	0
Chance 1 b	4-4		25 4	2-3		5-3					4	1	0	9	1	1
M Carthy c f		4-3	61 5 H		F.5		B-3				4	1	1	0	0	1
Kling C		2-3	2-3		6-4 H		5-3				4	0	1	1	2	0
Evers 2 b		2-3	8-4 H		FC		4-3				4	0	1	5	4	1
Tinker s s			86	F-1	F.7			5-4 z			3	0	0	2	2	0
Barry r f			z	2-3		5-3		FC			3	0	0	4	7	0
Brown Lundgren Reisea Weimer P			K		K		F-7				3	0	0	0	2	0
TOTAL	0	0	0	3	1	0	0	0	0		32	3	4	27	14	3

*Early Harry M.
Stevens scorecard,
the Polo Grounds,
1904. Note Tinker,
Evers, and Chance
on the Chicago
roster. (Collection
of Ron Menchine)*

they played the game "with relish." The act of showing off—showboating—is sometimes called "hotdogging."

In retrospect, it seems as though Stevens had a penchant for touching on things that became American metaphors. The scorecard itself became metaphoric of social and marital status—as in "note this engagement on your scorecard"—and to "not know the score," over time, became a way of being thought of as dumb or stupid. To score in a social context has taken on a meaning of its own, and if you don't think this came from baseball, then you have never heard of a person getting to first base (which is where you have to go before you can score.)

"Get your scorecard! You can't tell the players without a scorecard," Stevens's slogan, spread like wildfire. It outlasted Stevens, who passed away in 1934, and is now used in other sports and in other walks of life. Walk into a congressional hearing room, as the author has done, and you are likely to hear an aide handing out a list of witnesses to appear before the committee, using Stevens's selling call as he or she does so.

But perhaps the greatest of all scoring metaphors is contained in Grantland Rice's verse:

For when the One Great Scorer comes
To write against your name,
He marks not that you won or lost,
But how you played the Game.

This original version (modified over time by Rice and others), written in testimony to athletes at Vanderbilt University, was titled in its first version "Alumni Football." In his biography of Rice, *Sportswriter*, Charles Fountain notes that the line is still being chiseled into the stone facades of high-school gymnasiums and is still used by Little League parents who must tend to youngsters disconsolate over the loss of a game. When Carl Yastrzemski was inducted into the Baseball Hall of Fame in 1989, he said that he was most proud of the fact that he could look back on his career and say that he had lived up to the ideal of Rice's words. Charles Fountain put the significance of Rice's most recalled words in this way: "One hundred years from now, two hundred years from now, for as long as sport is played in America, the phrase will remain, for however tattered and frayed it might become, there is a gentleness, a lesson, a relevance in the words that is timeless."

N IS FOR NUMBERS, THE

Baseball fans love numbers. They love to swirl them around in their mouths like Bordeaux wine.
—*Pat Conroy,* Sport, *1979*

Baseball is neck-deep in numbers, but most of us need only a few statistics for survival and sanity. Here are the basics, and how they are computed.

Batting Average, Individual. Measures how often a batter gets a hit. Divide the total number of hits a player has made by the number of official times he has been at bat (walks, sacrifices, getting hit by a pitch, and being awarded first base via obstruction do not count as official at bats, but reaching base on an error does). Thus, a player with 32 hits in 110 official at bats is hitting .291.

Earned Run Average. Measures the average number of earned runs that a pitcher would give up if he pitched a complete nine-inning game (seven in softball). The number of earned runs a pitcher has allowed is multiplied by nine, or seven in softball. The answer is then divided by the actual number of innings the pitcher has pitched. A pitcher knocked out after 5 innings, having allowed 6 earned runs, would have an ERA for that game of 10.80. Unearned runs are ignored in this compilation: runs scored directly because of an error or catcher interference, or following an error on a play that would have ended the inning. More specifically, a run is unearned if scored by a runner who either got to first because of an error or whose life as a runner was extended by an error, if such a runner would have been put out by an errorless play.

Games Behind. Determined by adding the difference in wins between a trailing team and the leader to the difference in losses, and dividing by two. It is expressed as a combination of whole and half numbers. Thus, a team with a 52–46 record trails a team whose mark is 66–35 by 12 ½ games. Another way of defining this gap is to note that the team behind would have to defeat its rival 12 ½ straight times in head-to-head competition to gain a tie.

On-Base Percentage. The measure of an individual's ability to get on base. Total the number of times a player has gotten on base through hits, walks, or hit by pitches, but *not* by errors. Divide this total by the number of times a player has been at bat. A player with 100 at bats, 28 hits, 12 walks, and one hit by pitch would have an on-base percentage of .410.

Slugging Average / Slugging Percentage. Measures an individual's ability to get extra-base hits. Divide the total bases a player has accumulated through his own hits by the total number of times a player has been at bat. A batter with a triple, double, and single (6 total bases) in 12 at bats averages .500. During the 1920 season, Babe Ruth's slugging average was an astonishing .847 (388 bases in 458 at bats).

Production. A sophisticated measure of batting prowess created by simply adding On-Base Percentage and Slugging Average.

Stolen-Base Percentage. Determined by dividing successful stolen bases by stolen-base attempts.

Winning Percentage. Total up a pitcher's wins and losses to find his total decisions and then divide his wins by his decisions.

O IS FOR THE OFFICIAL SCORER

No 36-inch bat ever made as many hits as the scorer's little pencil.
—*Richard McAnn, in* For Men *magazine, August 1939*

Their names do not show up in programs, they are never, ever, seen on the field, and they are seldom mentioned in newspaper accounts of a game; but they are often booed and they only get recognition in times of controversy.

Under *no* circumstances can they override the umpire, and there is no circumstance in which they can affect the outcome of a game. The going rate for scoring a game is $75.00, paid by the home team.

Yet the official scorer plays a central role, essentially that of a baseball bookkeeper who at key moments must make a decision about how something is labeled in the official record. Often termed the "doorman to the Hall of Fame," the offi-

Leo "The Lip" Durocher in a typically expressive pose from a New York Giants scorecard, 1949. (Collection of Ron Menchine)

----

cial scorer has had tremendous influence over individual records. After all, one ruling can kill a batting title for one man and give it to another, and one call can make the difference between a no-hit ball game and a one-hitter.

Batting titles have been decided by the scorer's decision or indecision. Bob Addie, a sportswriter who often scored for the Washington Senators, recalled

such an incident in his memoirs, *Sportswriter*. In mid-August 1953, he was scoring a series at Griffith Stadium when Mickey Vernon of the Senators hit a hard grounder to Phil Rizzuto of the Yankees. Addie called it an error on Rizzuto.

"But the next day," Addie recalled in his book, "second base umpire Art Passarella told me the ball had taken a bad hop. 'I don't care about getting the error,'

Rizzuto said, 'but I would hate to rob a good guy like Mickey Vernon of a hit.'

"So I changed it to a hit—as we were always permitted to do before sending in the official score. That hit proved the difference between winning and losing the American League batting title in 1953 when Vernon beat out Cleveland's Al Rosen by one percentage point—.337 to .336. Actually the difference was two ten-thousandths of a point."

Addie added, "The next spring Vernon held out for a raise and owner Griffith blamed me for making it possible."

For most of this century, official scorers were exclusively members of the press and, as such, were especially reviled; most of them who ever went public complained that their chosen calling in the national pastime was misunderstood, unappreciated, and a magnet for criticism. And just about everyone has an idea as to someone who could do it better. One idea that has been kicking around for years is that of a "fifth umpire" who would do the job.

There have been many suggestions. In the late 1940s and early 1950s, Laraine Day, film actress and wife of New York Giants manager Leo Durocher, had her own television show preceding the team's games in New York, onto which she invited guests to discuss baseball and got to express her opinions on the game. Day was a knowledgeable fan who adored controversy. She was called a Red for questioning the playing of the national anthem at *every* sporting event—"When you hear it at every ballgame, prizefight and wrestling match, the edge is taken off and it becomes commonplace" was about the most offensive thing she said—and even got the various pre-union player representatives mad at her when she opposed the "reserve clause." Speaking of unions, before they were on anyone's agenda she came out against the idea of player's unions, invoking the wrath of organized labor.

Day really dropped a bomb when she advocated using ex-players as official scorers as opposed to the sportswriters who, in her words, "pass the honor around among themselves." To make matters worse, she brought her husband on the show to underscore the point. "There are certain tricky balls that scorers invariably charge as errors but which really should be hits," he said. "There are other balls that look hard and should be handled easily. I think the players would be far better satisfied if they had an old player doing the judging."

To those who insisted that only those who had played the game should score it, writer and scorer Dick Young replied, "I never laid an egg either, but I know a rotten one when I smell it." And as late as 1970 C. C. Johnson Spink could note in *The Sporting News* that "baseball alone, of all the major sports, puts the scoring burden on the sportswriters."

But in recent years an increasing number of major newspapers have decided that there is a conflict in using reporters as official scorers—who in the words of writer Jack Mann "are paid money by the enterprise he is paid to criticize"—and use instead someone from the outside who embraces it as an ill-paid part-time job that gets him or her closer to the game. Reporter or school teacher, the official scorer must have thick skin; he or she is, in fact, almost always in hot water with someone.

Some players, however, deserve a place in the scorers' Hall of Fame, reserved for those who can register disagreement without rancor. One of the most graceful examples took place in 1961 during a Los Angeles Dodgers home game against the St. Louis Cardinals. In one of the games Dodger slugger Duke Snider ripped a high line drive at second baseman Julian Javier of the Cards. Javier knocked the ball to the ground, retrieved it, and made a poor peg to first, allowing Snider to get on. Frank Finch, a reporter for the Los Angeles *Times*, who was the official scorer, called it an error. The assembled Dodger fans roared with disapproval, and neither Snider nor Javier was happy with the call either.

Writing about his decision later in *The Sporting News*, Finch reasoned, "While the ball was hit ferociously and Javier went beyond 'ordinary effort' in trying to catch it, I felt that he still had ample time to throw out Snider."

He added, "To Snider's everlasting credit, he let the matter drop after discussing the call with me the following day—without a semblance of rancor, I might add."

As it turned out, Snider ended the season with a .296 batting average, which would have been .300 with one more hit.

P IS FOR PROVING THE OFFICIAL BOX SCORE

A box score is in balance when the total of the team's times at bat, bases on balls received, hit batters, sacrifice bunts, sacrifice flies, and batters awarded first base because of interference or obstruction, equals the totals of that team's runs, players left on base, and the opposing team's putouts.
—The "formula" that all official scorers must learn by heart. It appears on the forms that are used to send in the final record of each game.

One of the duties of the official scorer is to prove the official box score—the one that becomes part of the official record—at the end of a game. It is the final check to make sure that it all balances—that the game is ready to go into the books. If the box score doesn't "prove," an error in scoring has occurred.

For the fan, proving one's own scorecard is an added bit of perfection. At the top of page 69 is a form for proof that has wide application in organized baseball, the amateur game, and softball. For your *scorecard* to "prove," each team's totals should be equal.

While always important, proofs become more so when a game is unusual and the numbers are high. One proof in the Hall of Fame collection, reproduced at the bottom of page 69, shows how the system works. It was for an International League game played on August 13, 1950 with Rochester hosting Jersey City. The game lasted 22 innings, and Rochester won 3–2. What made the game unusual is that both pitchers went the distance.

BOX-SCORE PROOF

Runs _____		At Bat _____	
LOB _____		Base on Balls _____	
		Sacrifices _____	
Opponents'		Hit by Pitcher & 1st by	
Putouts _____		Interference _____	
TOTAL _____		TOTAL _____	

BOX-SCORE PROOF

Visiting Club—Jersey City

Runs	2	At Bat	73
LOB	11	Base on Balls	5
		Sacrifices	1
Opponents'		Hit by Pitcher & 1st by	
Putouts	66	Interference	0
TOTAL	79	TOTAL	79

Home Club—Rochester

Runs	3	At Bat	72
LOB	17	Base on Balls	10
		Sacrifices	1
Opponents'		Hit by Pitcher & 1st by	
Putouts	63	Interference	0
TOTAL	83	TOTAL	83

Q IS FOR QUESTIONS FOR AND ANSWERS FROM THE OFFICIAL SCORER

Every club should have its regularly appointed scorer, and he should be one who fully understands every point of the game, and a person, too, of sufficient power of observation to note down correctly the details of every inning of the game.
—Beadle's Baseball Player, 1861

Ed Munson has two offices. One is in Fullerton, where he runs Creative Advertising, his public relations and advertising business, and the other is in a small open corner of the California Angels press box, where he scores all the home games.

The Anaheim space is tiny and sparse. To his left is a television monitor for replays, a space reserved for soft drinks, and score-books from earlier games. To his right within arm's length is a well-thumbed copy of the Official Baseball Rules, a small jar of Wite-Out, two spiral-bound scorebooks, and two Pentel marking pens.

Munson started in the Angels' public relations office, served as publicity director and traveling secretary, and then worked for Charlie Finley's Oakland A's for a season. Out of baseball from 1978 to 1980, Munson came back to Oakland as the official scorer for the final game of the 1980 season. In 1981, he was appointed full-time official scorer for the Angels at the urging of former Dodger pitcher and sportscaster Don Drysdale, a position he has held ever since. He came on the scene as more and more clubs and newspapers were phasing out sportswriters as official scorers.

Through the end of the 1995 season Munson had scored well over a thousand games. As official scorer, he had seen—and recorded—something on the order of 260,000 pitches and 20,000 outs. He estimates that he has assigned 850 errors. "As an official scorer, I got to see Reggie Jackson's 500th home run, Rod Carew's 3,000th hit, Don Sutton's 300th win," is one line from Ed Munson's baseball résumé.

What goes through the mind of a scorer?

Squabbles. With the advent of free agency in 1976 and bigger and bigger salaries, Munson believes, came the widespread general presumption of conflict between players and the official scorer. This made it even more difficult for a writer/official scorer to walk into the clubhouse after the game to gather quotes—as Munson puts it, "with a target on his back."

He adds: "I have twenty-four hours in which to change my mind, and I will listen to a player. I would say that ninety-eight percent of the people who call me on plays are respectful. I have never been cussed out by a player."

Fairness. His desire to be fair and withstand the pressure of being official scorer was difficult for Munson to deal with at first, but he came to realize that everyone who comes to or listens to a game has a stake in it. Judgment enters into a manager's mind, an umpire's mind, a player's mind, a fan's mind, and it is his job to be as fair as possible and to take other people's opinion into account.

Pressure. As much as he loves his job as official scorer, Munson admits that there are times of pressure. He recalls seven games in 1986 in which a no-hitter was taken into the

seventh inning in Anaheim. "Getting that far gets everyone edgy, and for the official scorer you want that first hit to be an obvious one . . . you want to make the right call."

Toughest decisions? Slow hoppers, usually to short, and in-betweeners. "I try to look at it this way: 'Would I accept an error if I were out there?' "

Criteria. "I use the concept of ordinary effort in judging errors and give the benefit of the doubt to the batter—not the fielder. This is what the rules call for . . . To some extent, I take the individual into account. Ordinary effort from an older player or one with many injuries may differ from ordinary effort from a man in perfect physical condition."

R IS FOR RULES OF THUMB

A hundred years ago, people used rules of thumb to make up for a lack of facts. Modern day rule of thumbing is rooted in an overabundance of facts.
—*Tom Parker, in his book*
Rules of Thumb

71

Baseball has two rule books: the official one, and the unwritten body of accumulated knowledge, also known as "the book," which tells you, for example, to hit behind the runner at first base and to never mention a no-hitter in progress.

Using both sets of rules—official and unwritten—as a guide, here are some points that can make you an expert scorer regardless of what system you use.

- If you keep track of putouts and assists, remember that in a rundown a fielder can be credited with only one assist no matter how many times he touches the ball.
- A batter is credited with batting in a run if he is put out, but not if the run scores as he hits into a double play.
- No error is charged on failure to complete a double play unless a runner advances as a result of the poor ball handling.
- A dropped third strike, and a throw to first for the out, gives the pitcher a strikeout (K), the catcher an assist, and the first baseman the putout.
- When a fourth ball hits the batter, it is scored as a hit-by-pitcher, not a base on balls.
- Fielders may be penalized with errors of omission as well as commission. For example, a pitcher failing to cover first base on an obvious play may be charged with an error. It

is rare, but fair. And it should be indicated by the scorer.

- Just because a player does not touch the ball does not exonerate him from being credited with an error. Consider the case of an easy ground ball going through a fielder's legs untouched.
- According to the rules, all that is required of a fielder to avoid an error is to expend "ordinary effort."
- A run is *unearned* if scored after the defense has failed in any or all chances to retire the side.
- Intent to interfere has nothing to do with charging interference; all that matters is whether or not interference took place.
- Rules don't cover everything. When they don't, custom—or convention—dictates. For instance, baseball writer and historian Bob Broeg wrote in a 1978 article on scoring: "There's a general rule of scoring thumb, also sound and sensible, that in the late innings of a hitless game, the pitcher be given the edge and that, therefore, the first hit against him, if any, be indisputably a clean one."
- A dropped fly ball that has been "lost in the sun" or "lost in the lights" will, in almost all cases, yield a hit for the batter, not an error—although there is nothing in the rule book on this.

- Then there is Maury Allen's Rule, which appeared under the writer/scorer's byline in *The Sporting News* in 1972: "Scoring is one-tenth judgment, one-tenth experience and eight-tenths common sense."

S IS FOR SCORECARDS AND SCOREBOOKS

----

*We arrive at the ballpark early . . .
and settle with score cards and
Cracker Jack and peanuts and
Schlitz and hot dogs. There is a
rasp in our voice, there is glory in
our infant heart, there is mustard
on our T-shirt.*
—*Donald Hall, in* Fathers
Playing Catch with Sons

"It is hard for me to imagine anyone, on a frosty December evening, sitting before the fire with the scorecard of a game played the previous June, and recreating the game, batter by batter and inning by inning," wrote Fred Schwed, Jr., in his 1957 book *How to Watch a Baseball Game*.

Nonetheless, there is ample evidence that many fans revisit games, including those played in 1957, on winter nights. Some bask in the replaying of a particular game; others review them in bulk looking for patterns and trends.

The question is how to best record games for future reference. Consider the very first words of *Pure Baseball* by Keith Hernandez and Mike Bryan: "First, I'd like to see you buy a real scorebook that has a place to chart the balls and strikes. The little scoresheet they print on page 37 of the official program just isn't good enough for the advanced fan. If you really want to get into baseball, you have to follow the game pitch by pitch."

Here is my opinion. For those who are going to spend a lot of time with their scoring after the game, having all of one's games in one book makes sense. For those who relish the nostalgia of having been there, it is hard to beat the scorecard that you buy from a vendor on game day.

Then there is the question of those scorebooks with preprinted notations that come in a wild array of designs and variations.

Some fans and scorers swear by them (usually adding that some are better than others), while others don't like them at all. In his 1986 *Baseball Abstract* Bill James, collectively, gives them a less than rave review. "There must be a hundred or more scoresheet forms in use around the coun-

73

try, and many of them, to be honest, are just confusing." James talks about the form that uses little boxes divided into four parts representing the four bases, the many systems that use a little diamond drawn in broken lines and a multiple-choice quiz in the corner of each box, and the "dreadful" one with a honeycomb pattern in green ink and little numbers printed around it.

James argues that they all lay "way too much" ink on the page before you start trying to make an account of the game. The other problem is that they make room for every batter to hit in every inning, thereby making the resulting spaces so small "that you can't hardly get anything in there."

In his book *The Scorekeeper's Friend—The Most Complete Source of Instruction, Reference and Support for Baseball and Softball Scorekeepers*, Bill Glasco, who also produces his own grid—GAMETIME Basic Scorebook—acknowledges that some of James's criticism is valid. Nevertheless, Glasco's grid is fairly easy to master and allows for the scorer to track each batter's count as well as his hits.

Again this is a matter of personal preference and to some degree follows the needs of the scorer. When I was scoring recreational league games for my son's coaches, I really liked having the predrawn diamond in the scorebook. Being

able to indicate with a line on the diamond where a hit ball traveled was important information for the manager. If an opposing batter had hit two balls to right center, the manager could position the field for his third time at bat.

T IS FOR TEAM ERROR

New York, N.Y.—The "team error," a concept new to baseball, has been proposed by the Baseball Writers' Association of America. No specific plan for exact definition of "team error" is being advocated by the writers: they just want the Scoring Rules Committee to accept the principle that, in some situations, charging one player with an error is unjust, and to explore ways to define a team error is to take care of those situations.
—Leonard Koppett, The Sporting News, *August 22, 1970*

Many baseball writers, official scorers, and others embrace the principle of the "team error," which was first proposed by the Baseball Writers' Association in 1970 and nixed by the Official Playing Rules Committee.

There are several situations in which it would be assigned, but this one illustrates the point nicely. A batter hits a high, soft fly ball. The second baseman and the right fielder both go after the ball, they collide, and the ball hits the ground. By custom this is scored as a hit— just as it would be if the two players let the ball drop while avoiding collision: neither of the two individual fielders is charged with an error, but the pitcher is charged with giving up a hit, even though he got the batter to pop up.

Writer Leonard Koppett advocated the "team error" in his 1970 article in *The Sporting News*: "Now, the injustice done to a player's batting average or a fielder's record is relatively slight—but the potential damage to a pitcher's earned run average can be disastrous." Koppett was picking up on the team error idea, which writer Dick Young had embraced as his pet project years earlier.

Here's another good example of the usefulness of the team error. There is a runner on first. The right fielder scoops up a single and throws it (accurately) to third on one bounce; however, it hits the runner sliding in and bounces away. Both runners get an extra base and the right fielder, according to the rules, is given an error, even though he made a good play. The pitcher's record is protected, but the fielder's is not. A team error would preserve the pitcher's immunity from earned-run damage without giving the fielder an undeserved error.

In 1980, Paul MacFarlane of *The Sporting News* came across this interesting entry in a nineteenth century (1888) Reach Guide:

The Baseball Reporters Association on December 12, 1887, adopted the following scoring rule: "When a player reaches first base through an error of judgment, such as two fielders allowing the ball to drop between them, the batter shall not be credited with a base hit nor the fielder charged with an error. But it shall be scored as an unaccepted chance, and the batter shall be charged with a time at bat."

In other words, the team error concept is nothing new.

Despite the fact that this proposal lies in limbo, there is no reason why the individual scorer cannot adopt it.

U IS FOR UNCOVERING THE TRUTH OF THE HORSE'S TEETH

In the year of our Lord 1432, there arose a grievous quarrel among the brethren of a monastery over the number of teeth in the mouth of a horse. For thirteen days the disputation raged without ceasing. All the ancient books and chronicles were fetched out, and wonderful and ponderous erudition, such as was never before heard of in this region, was made manifest. At the beginning of the fourteenth day, a youthful friar of goodly bearing asked his learned superiors for permission to add a word.

Straightway, to the wonder of the disputants whose deep wisdom he sore vexed, he beseeched them to unbend in a manner coarse and unheard of, and to look in the mouth of a horse to find an answer to their questionings. At this their dignity being greatly hurt, they waxed exceeding wroth; and joining in a mighty uproar, they fell upon him, hip and thigh, and cast him out forthwith. For, said they, surely Satan hath tempted this bold neophyte to declare unholy and unheard of ways of finding truth contrary to all the teachings of the fathers!
—*Francis Bacon (1561–1626), quoted by Earnshaw Cook in* Percentage Baseball

----

Baseball's underpinning and much of its enjoyment is based on being able to count the teeth—actually being alert to the numbers and the nuances of actual play. Scoring helps us count the teeth, and so does reading the box score and the standings. Purists insist that the large mass of people who vote in the All-Star balloting *do not* count the teeth but are reacting to the presence and career impact of a player (and in some cases to local P.A. announcers who request that the fans stuff the ballot box for a local star).

But there are other ways to count the teeth, especially at the ballpark. One is batting practice, another comes from keeping a close eye on the bullpen, and the most important may be the scoreboard.

"Play the scoreboard" is the time-honored maxim of managers and coaches. What this means is that what is on the scoreboard—the score, the inning, the number of balls and strikes, and the men on base—dictates what you should and should not do.

The scoreboard is therefore an integral element of the game, with some of the following likely to come into play in any given game:

The fabled "exploding scoreboard" created for Bill Veeck in Chicago. Scorekeepers have been known to pay homage to this innovation by drawing small explosions on their scorecards for a spectacular play. (Chicago White Sox)

■ Both teams try to score as often as they can in the early innings but become more conservative—both offensively and defensively—as the game progresses.

■ Runners don't steal when their team is well ahead, or when it is two or more runs down.

■ In a tight divisional or wild-card race, the progress of out-of-town games on the scoreboard may dictate strategy.

The scoreboard also comes in handy for catchers who want to signal their pitchers without tipping off the opposition. In *Nine Innings*, Daniel Okrent describes one system called "scoreboard signing." In this case, if the count on the scoreboard was even, the third sign signaled by the catcher was the real sign (the first two being dummy signals). But if the batter was ahead in the count the second sign was the good one, and if the pitcher was ahead it was the first.

Of course, the scoreboard is where you learn how the official scorer ruled a play that could be an H or an E. Some ballparks have given this a creative/commercial angle, such as the SCHAEFER BEER sign that showed up in Ebbets Field after World War II and relayed the scorer's decision by lighting the H or E in SCHAEFER.

V IS FOR VEXATIOUS MOMENTS IN OFFICIAL SCORING HISTORY

It is an article of the ballplayer's faith that all newspapermen are purblind and mentally incompetent, and that the one currently doubling as official scorer is a troglodyte as well. As for the scorer in any rival city, he never gives one of our guys a break and probably is in the pay of a foreign power.
    —Red Smith, writing in the Mutual Baseball Almanac

----

1. Snuffy's Hit. Batting titles have been decided by the scorer's decision or indecision, as previously noted. One title that changed hands because of a scorer's reversal had a faint odor to it.

On the last day of the 1945 season a New York writer scored a ball hit by George "Snuffy"

Stirnweiss of the Yankees as an error. At the moment, Stirnweiss was battling Chicago's Tony Cuccinello for the batting average title, and as soon as it was realized that the error would deprive Stirnweiss of the title, the scorer changed the error to a hit. Stirnweiss won with .309; Cuccinello ended up with .308.

2. Two for Cobb. There have been moments, however, when the league president changed a ruling. Two of great note involved key records for Ty Cobb.

In 1910, Cobb and Larry Lajoie, the slugging second baseman for the Cleveland Indians, were neck-and-neck in their attempt to win the American League batting title until the very last week of the season, when Lajoie began to fade. When the Indians went into St. Louis for a doubleheader against the Browns on the last day of the season, Cobb's title was all but assured.

George "Snuffy"
Stirnweiss
(Author's collection)

In St. Louis, Lajoie went to bat eight times and was credited with eight hits, which at first glance suggested a tie but fell short by a fractional margin. But league president Ban Johnson smelled a rat and determined that the first "hit" had been a sinfully misjudged looping fly, "hit" number two was a badly played bounder to the shortstop, and the last were bunts hit down the third-base line. Johnson also discovered that Red Corriden, the Browns' rookie third baseman, had been instructed to play deep that day, although he knew that it would prevent him from handling bunts. Johnson not only corrected the record but ordered the immediate suspension of the Browns manager, Jack O'Connor, and Coach Harry Howell.

In 1922, in a game between Cobb's Tigers and the New York Yankees, the official scorer, John Kieran of the *New York Times*, had run for cover to avoid the rain that was falling in the open press

Ty Cobb in a rare moment of conviviality with the likable pitching great Walter Johnson. (Library of Congress)

box. At one point in the game, Cobb hit a grounder toward the shortstop, Everett Scott, who bobbled the muddy ball, allowing Cobb to reach first. From dry ground, Kieran signaled an error, but it was not seen in the press box. Fred Lieb of *The Sporting News*, who also filed game summaries to the Associated Press, decided that, taking Cobb's speed and the field conditions into consideration, there was no question that this was a hit. He never bothered to look in Kieran's direction and telegraphed it as such to the Associated Press, which sent it out as a hit in the afternoon box scores.

The discrepancy between the two rulings did not show up until the end of the season, when the league's official record showed Cobb batting .399 and the AP and Irwin Howe, the American League statistician who ran an unofficial statistics service, showed Cobb at .401.

Lieb sided with Kieran, on the principle that the official scorer is official and that if a decision could be reversed weeks later to award a man a higher batting average, there was no point in having a scorer. However, Ban Johnson awarded Cobb the hit—reversing his scorer and siding with Howe, his statistician—and gave the Georgia Peach his third season with an average of .400 or better. The Baseball Writers' Association, of which Lieb was president, sided with Kieran, and the 1923 baseball guides carried this notation with Ty Cobb's .401 for 1922: "Not recognized by the Baseball Writers' Association." Cobb still didn't win the American League batting title, as George Sisler hit .420.

The very next season Lieb was involved in what he later termed "the saddest decision I ever made." He prevented Howard Ehmke of the Red Sox from becoming the first pitcher to throw back-to-back no-hitters. Coming off a no-hitter, the first batter Ehmke faced against the Yankees in a September game was Whitey Witt. The swift Witt chopped a ball down to third that took an odd hop and was muffled against the chest of outfielder-turned-infielder Howard Shanks. By the time he got the ball into his hand he saw that it was too late to get Witt and held on to it. As official scorer, Lieb felt that Witt's hard-earned reputation as the fastest base runner in the league—and the odd hop taken by the chopped ball—earned him a hit, and it was carried as such in the early editions of the newspapers. Nobody in the press box objected.

Ehmke did not allow another hit, and as the innings passed the pressure began to build on Lieb to reverse his decision. He stuck to his guns even through an immediate public outcry followed by a petition drive initiated by fans pleading to have the league president reverse the ruling.

Lieb later admitted that his call was doubtful and that he might have scored the same play an error in a later inning of the game with a no-hitter on the line. In his autobiography, *Baseball As I Have Known It*, Lieb said that the reason he was so obstinate dated back to 1912 and a conversation he had had with Tom Lynch, president of the National League, who was also known as "king of the umpires." The day before the two men talked, a scorer had changed a hit to an error in order to give Jeff Tesreau of the Giants a no-hitter. Lynch was very upset by the change in scoring and said to Lieb, "Be like an umpire. He can't be influenced by anyone to change a decision he made in the second inning. Whether right or wrong, it was his honest judgment. As a scorer, hold your ground the same way. I don't like no-hitters that are scored in the clubhouse."

Not everyone has been as principled as Lieb.

3. Reversals. The most noted (and notorious) reversals in scoring history relate to no-hitters. In 1917, Ernie Koob of the old St. Louis Browns was given a no-hitter when an early-inning hit call was turned into an error; Virgil Trucks, pitching for Detroit, got a no-hitter under the same conditions.

On Opening Day of the 1936 season, with the President of the United States, Franklin D.

Roosevelt, in the VIP box, Washington pitcher Buck Newsom began the fifth inning by directing a self-satisfied grin at the President. To that point, Newsom had not allowed a hit to the New York Yankees.

The first pitch to Ben Chapman was a strike, and the second pitch was a fastball inside that Chapman stabbed at and sent slowly down the third-base line. Newsom ran over to field the bunt, but it skidded past him. Ossie Bluege, playing third base, charged the ball, scooped it up, and fired it toward first base. The ball never got there; it collided loudly with the back of Newsom's head and bounced back to Bluege, who fielded it for the second time. Chapman was safe before the second throw to first arrived.

Was it a hit or an error, and if an error, who committed it? Writer Francis E. Stan was in the box that day as official scorer, and he signaled a hit be credited to Chapman. So it was that Buck Newsom lost his bid for an Opening Day no-hitter in front of the President of the United States. Stan's decision was loudly hooted, and it was appealed to the president of the league, who upheld Stan.

4. Press-Baiter. In the mid-1930s Joe Kuhel of the old Washington Senators was so incensed after having been charged with an error that he

took a swing at sportswriter Shirley Povich when Povich entered the clubhouse at the end of the game. Povich protested that Bob Considine had been the official scorer that day.

Senators owner Clark Griffith fined Kuhel $100 for the incident, and three days later Kuhel got a letter from a fan: "Here's $50 to pay half of your fine for taking a swing at Povich. I'd have sent you the other half if you hadn't missed."

5. One for the Books. Mike Schmidt's final career at bat was ruled an error, not a hit, and there was pressure to change the ruling. The official scorer was Mike Lefkow, a reporter for the Contra Costa *Times*, who had time to change the decision but stuck to his guns. He later said: "Because it was Mike Schmidt, I talked to a few people who had more experience scoring games, and they said you don't change a decision for that reason. I do understand the historical essence, though."

W IS FOR WRITING INSTRUMENTS

Assigned the job of scorekeeper in a game at Morristown, Ohio, one day in 1902, a young man named Stanton Walker found that his pencil needed sharpening in one of the late innings. He asked the man sitting next to him for a knife. Walker had just started to put a new point on his pencil when a hard foul ball shot off the plate, struck his hand, and drove the blade of the knife into his heart.
—*From* Low and Inside, *the incomparable collection of baseball anecdotes and oddments written by Ira L. Smith and H. Allen Smith*

Underscored by this sad cautionary tale is the conclusion that one should not bring any writing instrument to the ballpark that needs to be sharpened.

You have two options: (1) a good sturdy mechanical pencil or pencils #2 or darker with eraser (important if you ever want to photocopy your work), or (2) a pen. Unless you have superior eyesight and don't mind a lapful of tiny lead fragments, you will probably want to steer clear of those dainty mechanical pencils with the angel-hair lead. The same goes for those goofy little eraserless golf pencils that some of the teams issue (or sell) with the purchase of a scorecard. They could only have been offered for the purpose of scoring by someone who has never scored a game. Many broadcasters use ballpoint pens, because they are easier to read in the usually dim light of the broadcast booth.

X IS FOR X'S AND CHECKS

When the count reaches 0–2 or 2–0—that's when the player's ears start to prick . . .
—*Thomas Boswell*

Few scorers record every pitch, because it simply takes too much concentration and time. However, there is a fallback position that was first suggested by writer Thomas Boswell in a 1979 article on scoring.

He suggests using a corner of the scoring block—or the summary columns at the right of the scorecard, if you don't plan to fill them in—to record two important items:

(1) The batter's final count: if it's one and one when he gets a hit in his first at bat, write 1:1 in the block or first box in the summary columns.

(2) The pitcher's effectiveness: if the count reaches 0–2 or 2–0, put a check ✓ or ✗ in the block or box. The 0–2 check mark is a mark of success for the pitcher, but the 2–0 ✗ is a mark of failure.

Without turning into an accountant, the scorer now has a much better sense of the war between the mound and the plate, or as Boswell put it originally, "to sense where the initiative and the worry reside." This system gives the scorer the number of balls thrown by each pitcher and the ratio of strikes to balls. As for the checks and ✗'s they should, excepting flukes, point the way, respectively, to victory or doom.

Y IS FOR YEAR-BY-YEAR TIMELINE OF SCORING RULE CHANGES

The scoring rules are at the heart of baseball's accountability to itself and the millions of fans who follow the game day by day.
—*Dennis Bingham and Thomas R. Heitz, in* Total Baseball, *Third Edition*

To a great extent, scoring rules determine the records and who holds them. Here is a brief account of how the rules that govern scoring have changed over the years. It summarizes highlights; anyone wanting to consult each and every rule change would be advised to consult *Total Baseball* by John Thorn, Pete Palmer, and Michael Gershman.

1858. The first mention of the official scorer in the rule book. Two "recorders" were called for, one from each of the contending clubs.

85

1860. Umpires begin calling balls and strikes to speed up play.

1863. Henry Chadwick's box-scoring system is adopted, thereby making baseball the best recorded of all games.

1877. A base on balls is no longer charged as an at bat, which it had been prior to this season.

1883. An error is assessed the pitcher for a walk, balk, wild pitch, or hit batter. An error is charged to the catcher for a passed ball.

1886. A hit batsman is not to be charged with an at bat. This was also the year in which the old custom of the batter being allowed to call for a high or low ball from the pitcher ended.

• No stolen base is to be credited to a runner for bases advanced on his or her own initiative, such as when he or she goes to third on a single.

1887. Bases on balls are scored as hits for this season only.

• The 1883 error rule is rescinded and "no error" is charged to the pitcher for a walk, balk, wild pitch, or hit batter, nor is the catcher assigned an error for a passed ball.

1888. Bases on balls are no longer scored as hits or counted as times at bat, owing to the inflated batting averages in 1887. Tip O'Neill topped the American Association with a .492 mark, while the National League's leader was Cap Anson at .421. In his book *The Rules of Baseball*, David Nemec notes that if the 1887 rule had been in effect in 1941, Ted Williams would have batted .540.

• The 1883 error rule—re-pealed in 1887—is brought back, meaning that an error is again charged to the pitcher for a walk, balk, wild pitch, or hit batter and the catcher again gets an error for a passed ball.

• A hit batsman is credited with a hit.

1889. Again no error is charged to the pitcher for a walk, balk, wild pitch, or hit batter.

• The sacrifice is recognized in

the statistics of the game. The batter, however, is still charged with an at bat.

1893. The batter credited with a sacrifice is not charged with an at bat.

- The pitching distance is moved to 60 feet, 6 inches.

1895. The foul tip is ruled a strike. This tended to shorten the time of a game.

1901. The American League comes into being and the "modern" era of baseball begins.

1908. A batter is not charged with an at bat on a sacrifice fly when a run scores after the catch of his fly ball.

1909. If a runner is thrown out on an attempted double steal, neither runner is credited with a stolen base.

- An unsuccessful bunt on the third strike is a K, and the catcher is credited with the putout.

1912. Earned runs are charged to pitchers.

1913. Pitchers are henceforth charged with the batters they leave on base. Prior to this the responsibil-

ity had been the relieving pitcher's. The rule was changed on the heels of Walter Johnson's losing his 16-game victory streak in 1912 when he entered in the seventh inning of a tie game to relieve a pitcher who had left two men on base, allowed one of the two base runners he had inherited to score the winning run, and thereby became the losing pitcher. The scorer's decision was upheld by Ban Johnson and the loss held. Johnson shares the American League record for consecutive wins with three others—Smoky Joe Wood, Lefty Grove, and Schoolboy Rowe.

1920. The RBI becomes an official statistic of baseball (although many sportswriters had kept prior track of them on an informal basis).

- Game-ending home runs are now scored as home runs. Prior to 1920 a ball hit out of the park for a home run was only good for the runs needed for a one-run margin. This cost Frank "Home Run"

Baker three homers in 1919, of which two were grand slams. Babe Ruth reaped the benefit of the new rule.

• No stolen base is credited when the defense makes no attempt to get the runner out.

• A player must appear in 100 games to be eligible for the batting and slugging title.

1926. The sacrifice-fly rule is amended so that the batter is not charged with an at bat if a runner advances a base.

• Pitchers are not credited with a K if a batter reaches first because of a wild pitch on the third strike.

1931. The 1926 sacrifice-fly rule is repealed and the scored sacrifice disappears.

1939. The sacrifice-fly rule comes back for one season, but it is repealed the following year.

1945. A batter must have at least 400 at bats to qualify for the batting or slugging crowns.

1950. The official scorer is first accredited as representing the league in the rule book, although he/she

had been long recognized as such. Beginning in the 1860s, organized baseball had had official scorers whose authority was granted by the league.

• For this season only, a player must play in at least two-thirds of his team's scheduled games to qualify for the batting and slugging championships. The next year, the 400 at bats minimum was restored.

1954. Any outfield fly that scores a run is counted as a sacrifice. This helps give slight increases to batting averages. Previously the sacrifice had to have been deliberate and successful.

1957. League presidents are first required by rule to appoint official scorers.

1967. To qualify for the league batting or slugging title, a player must have a total of at least 3.1 plate appearances for every scheduled game.

1969. Organized baseball accepts the "save" as a pitching statistic.

• Runs are earned against a

relief pitcher who enters the game in the middle of an inning as if he entered the game at the beginning of the inning.

1973. A reliever gets a save for protecting a lead, no matter how high the score.

• The designated hitter (DH) rule becomes an option, but only the American League adopts it.

1974. Scorer-baiting in the National League reaches such a level that league president Chub Feeney issues a warning against it.

• The save rule is again amended. No save is to be credited to a relief pitcher unless he faces the tying run on base or at the plate, or unless he pitches three effective innings.

1975. Once again the save rule is changed. Now if the tying run is on deck when the reliever arrives, he may still earn a save.

1976. The name of a pitcher credited with a save is to be shown in the scoring summary.

1979. The official scorer must make all decisions concerning judgment calls within twenty-four hours of a game's being officially completed.

1980. Game-winning RBI (GWRBI) are officially credited, for the RBI that gives a team a lead that it never relinquishes.

1981. The Year of the Asterisk, so called because of the disorienting effects on statistics of a players' strike.

1983. A pitcher's ERA is henceforth calculated with fractions of innings pitched rather than only with full innings, as before.

1989. The game-winning RBI (GWRBI) is dropped from the rule book and by most newspapers. It is argued widely that the statistic in many cases is irrelevant. For example, your team wins 12–0, and the GWRBI goes to the player who brought in the first run.

1994. The season ends prematurely, eliminating final standings, playoffs, and the World Series, and posting records that will forever remain under the shadow of a season that was never allowed to play to its time-honored conclusion.

Z IS FOR ZAMBONI ON FIELD AND OTHER ZANY (BUT RELEVANT) SCORING NOTATIONS

----

*Richard Mark (American)/
Wayne Messmer (Canadian).
—National anthem notations
in Warner Fusselle's 1990 All-
Star scoring*

Finally, it must be stated that the only limit to what belongs on one's scorecard is one's imagination.

Who sang the national anthem, the temperature at game time, the direction and intensity of the wind, are all potentially relevant. Looking at Warner Fusselle's 1990 All-Star score sheet, one can find out that the wind was blowing in at 16 mph, that 39,071 were at the game, and that the game took 2 hours and 53 minutes to play and much, much more.

As for printed scorecards, one of the innovative features of *Outside Pitch*, an unofficial scorecard and program sold outside Camden Yards in Baltimore, is that the player rosters contain player salaries. Watching Mike Mussina pitch a doozy in 1994 while Sid Fernandez, then on the Orioles staff, languished on the Disabled List, it was noteworthy to see that Mussina's salary was $750,000 a year while Fernandez's annual take was $3,333,333.

Sportswriter Red Barber loved to tell of colleague Henry McLemore, whose wife created a set of immense score sheets for the 1938 World Series with the classic notation HWHI for "He walked him intentionally."

In his autobiography, sportscaster Lindsey Nelson tells of his severely retarded and much-loved daughter Sharon, who followed the Mets and enjoyed scoring immensely. "Well," wrote Nelson, "I looked at Sharon's scorecard one day and discovered that after each player, in its proper order and inning, there was a neat zero. This seemed like an odd scoring system to me, and I inquired. Sharon patiently explained to her unlettered father, 'It means that he has been here and is gone.' I suppose that's as good a scoring system as any. It's important, I think, to know who has been here and is gone."

The most noteworthy zany notation of all belongs to none other than Hall of Famer

Creative score-keeping comes into play when the unusual occurs. This bench-clearing brawl from a July 1939 contest between the Cubs and Giants is a case in point. You could use the notation BCB and the numbers of the players involved as a way of recording the event, or create your own symbol for a rhubarb. (Author's collection)

Phil Rizzuto, who invented and pioneered the use of WW in his scoring as a Yankee announcer. As Rizzuto has explained on numerous occasions, WW is for those moments he "wasn't watching."

Zamboni?

Trade name for a machine used to clean ice-hockey rinks and baseball fields sporting artificial grass. Should be noted when spotted.

Scorecard vendors cry, Chicago White Sox scorecard, 1952. (Collection of Ron Menchine)

SCORECARDS OF HISTORIC GAMES

$\mathcal{O}$ ne of the many pleasures of keeping score is the ability to recreate a game at a later date. This may be particularly satisfying if the game has been historic in some way—a no-hitter, a pennant clincher, a record setter, or the like. To make the point, this section reproduces the filled-in scorecards from seven historic games. Once you figure out the scorer's system, you'll quickly spot where Babe Ruth "called" his famous home run in the 1932 World Series, or the events of the memorable ninth inning culminated by Bobby Thomson's 1951 "shot heard round the world." These scorecards have never, to my knowledge, been reproduced before, and I am grateful to their owners for permitting their reproduction here; they are truly part of baseball's history.

Game program and scorecard kept by Giants' announcer Russ Hodges with his partner Ernie Harwell, of the final game of the 1951 playoff series between the New York Giants and the Brooklyn Dodgers. He clearly was so excited by Bobby Thomson's "shot heard round the world" that he failed to mark Thomson's game-winning home run and the final score on the scorecard; he did, however, sign it. (National Baseball Library, Cooperstown, N.Y.)

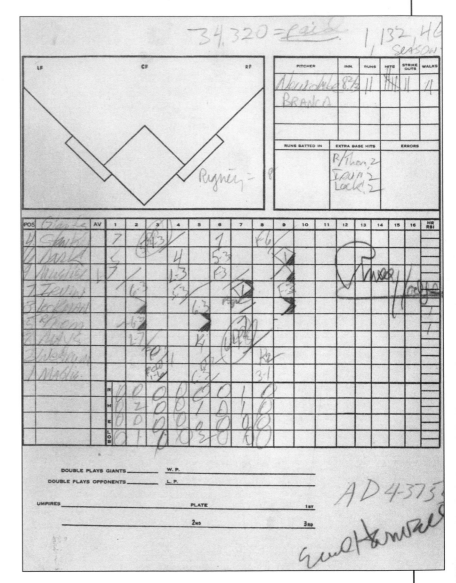

Scorecards from games by two of baseball's greatest pitchers: (Top) Nolan Ryan's 300th victory won by Texas over Milwaukee, 11–3 on July 31, 1990 (Collection of James L. Gates), and (bottom) Sandy Koufax's 1–0 no-hitter, September 9, 1965 vs. the Chicago Cubs. Note that he struck out the last six batters. (National Baseball Library, Cooperstown, N.Y.)

```
NEW YORK—AMERICAN.
                  Ab  R  BH  PO  A  E
Combs, cf .........5   1   0   1  0  0
Sewell, 3b ........2   1   0   2  2  0
Ruth, lf ..........4   2   2   2  0  0
Gehrig, 1b ........5   2   2  12  1  0
Lazzeri, 2b .......4   1   0   3  4  1
Dickey, c .........4   0   1   2  1  0
Chapman, rf .......4   0   2   0  0  0
Crosetti, ss ......4   0   1   4  4  0
Pipgras, p ........5   0   0   0  0  0
Pennock, p ........0   0   0   0  1  0

Totals ........37   7   8  27 13  1

CHICAGO—NATIONAL.
                  Ab  R  BH  PO  A  E
Herman, 2b ........4   1   0   1  2  1
English, 3b .......4   0   0   0  3  0
Cuyler, rf ........4   1   3   1  0  0
Stephenson, lf ....4   0   1   1  0  0
J. Moore, cf ......3   1   0   3  0  0
Grimm, 1b .........4   0   1   8  0  0
Hartnett, c .......4   1   1  10  1  1
Jurges, ss ........4   1   3   3  3  2
Root p ............2   0   0   0  3  0
Malone p ..........0   0   0   0  0  0
z—Gudat ..........1   0   0   0  0  0
May, p ............0   0   0   0  0  0
Tinning, p ........0   0   0   0  0  0
zz—Koenig ........0   0   0   0  0  0
zzz—Hemsley ......1   0   0   0  0  0

Totals .........35   5   9  27  9  4
```

z—Batted for Malone in 7th.
zz—Batted for Tinning in 9th.
zzz—Batted for Koenig in 9th.
Innings:
New York ....301 020 001—7
Chicago ....102 100 001—5
Runs batted in—Ruth, 4; Cuyler, 2; Gehrig, 2; Grimm, Chapman, Hartnett. Two-base hits—Cuyler, Grimm, Jurges, Chapman. Home runs—Ruth, 2; Gehrig, 2; Cuyler, Hartnett. Stolen bases—Jurges, Double plays—Sewell, Lazzeri and Gehrig; Herman, Jurges and Grimm. Left on bases—New York, 11; Chicago, 6. Base on balls—off Root, 3 (Sewell 2, Chapman), Malone 4, (Lazzeri, Dickey, Crosetti, Ruth); Pipgras 3 (Herman, Moore, English). Struck out—By Root, 4 (Lazzeri, Pipgras 2, Combs; Malone, 4 (Pipgras 2, Ruth, Chapman); May 1 (Combs). Tinning 1, (Pipgras). Hits and runs off Root, 6 hits, six runs in 4 1-3 innings. Off Malone, 1 hit, no runs in 2 2-3 innings. Off May, 1 hit, 1 run in 1 1-3 innings. Off Tinning, no hits, no runs, in 2-3 innings. Off Pipgras, 9 hits, 5 runs in 8 innings (none out in 9th). Off Pennock, no runs, no hits in one inning. Hit by pitcher, by May (Sewell). Losing pitcher, Root. Umpires—Van Graflan (A. L.) plate; Magerkurth (N. L.) first; Dinneen (A. L.) second; Klem (N. L.) third. Time of game, 2:11.

1932

CHICAGO CUBS
vs.
NEW YORK YANKEES

CHICAGO NATIONAL LEAGUE BALL CLUB

WRIGLEY FIELD

Souvenir SCORE CARD 25¢

WORLD'S SERIES

Game program (left), box score (right), and filled-in scorecard (facing page), from the 1932 World Series game in which Babe Ruth is alleged to have called his home run off Cubs' pitcher Charley Root. Ruth and Lou Gehrig each had two home runs that day; Ruth's "called shot" came in the 5th inning. The Yankees won the game and the World Series, but despite their talent, they wouldn't appear in another until 1936, Joe DiMaggio's rookie year. (Collection of Ron Menchine)

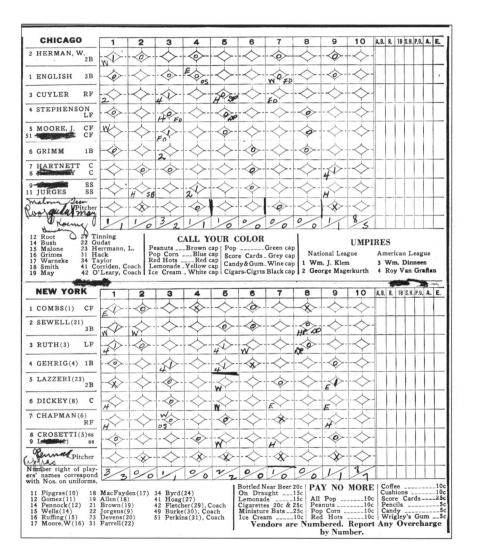

AT BAT 8 POS.
BALL 1 STRIKE 2 OUT

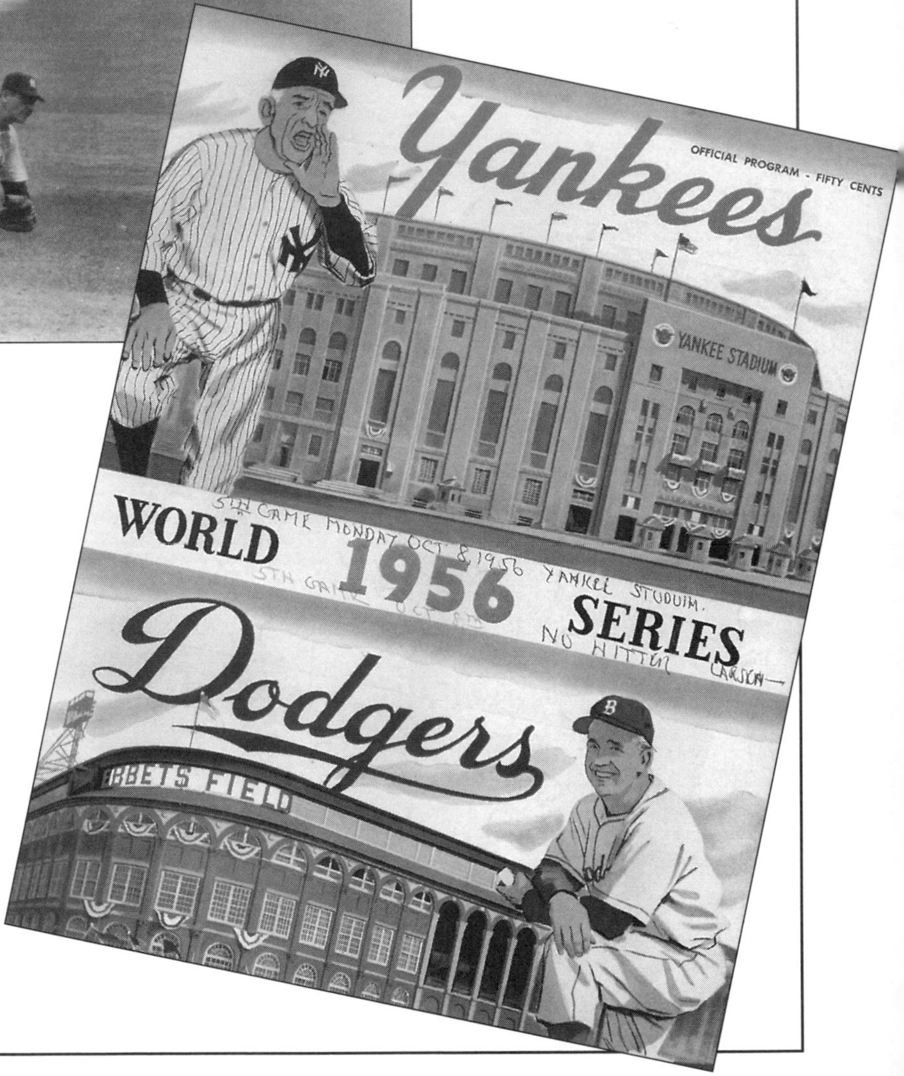
Yankees
OFFICIAL PROGRAM - FIFTY CENTS
YANKEE STADIUM
WORLD 1956 SERIES
5TH GAME MONDAY OCT 8, 1956 YANKEE STUDUIM.
NO HITTER
Dodgers
BBETS FIELD

BROOKLYN DODGERS

				1	2	3	4	5	6	7	8	9	10	AB	R	H	PO	A	E
19	GILLIAM	2B		P			4.3			6.3									
1	REESE	SS		K			4.3			4.8									
4	SNIDER	CF					K			4.7									
42	ROBINSON	3B			6.3		F.9			1.3									
14	HODGES	1B			K		4.8			5									
15	AMOROS	LF			4.4		4.3			4.8									
6	FURILLO	RF				F.9		F.4		F.4									
39	CAMPANELLA	C				K		F.4											
35	MAGLIE	P				F.8		K											

Earned runs	Three-base hits	Two-base hits	Runs batted in ....
Home runs	Left on bases	Sacrifices	Stolen bases ....
Hits off	Hit by pitcher	Bases on Balls	Strikeouts ....
Wild pitches	Time of game	Double plays	Passed balls ....

Game program (facing page) and filled-in scorecard from Don Larsen's perfect game in the 1956 World Series against the Brooklyn Dodgers. The photograph shows Larsen's final pitch on its way to the plate. Dick Casey, who scored the game was so excited that he forgot to score the last two batters: Roy Campanella grounded out to Billy Martin at second and Dale Mitchell, batting for pitcher Sal Maglie, took a called third strike to end the game. (Program: The Casey Collection of The Sports Museum of New England; photograph: the National Baseball Library, Cooperstown, N.Y.)

CINCINNATI AT NEW YORK

DEFENSE
YOUNGBLOOD 7th
MAZILLI

HENDERSON   MADDOX

FOLI   FLYNN

RANDALL   SWAN   MONTANEZ

STEARNS

	W	L	IP	HITS	SO	BB	GS	CG	ERA
STARTING	4	9	$108\frac{1}{3}$	134	50	39	18	1	5.33

PITCHER	IP	HITS	SO	BB	RUNS	ER	WP	HB	
HUME	$3\frac{1}{3}$	6	2	1	5	4	0	0	
BORBON	$2\frac{2}{3}$	2	0	1	0	0	0	0	BK
TOMLIN	2	4	1	1	4	4	1	0	

UMPIRES:
PLATE WEST
FIRST KIBLER
SECOND COLOSI
THIRD DAVIDSON
DATE 7/25/78
WEATHER
TEMP
WIND

TOTALS	R	H	E	LB
METS	9	12	0	6
REDS	2	7	3	5
WINNING PITCHER	SWAN		3	5
LOSING PITCHER	HUME		4	10
TIME OF GAME	2126 1907	2:19		
ATTENDANCE	44210			

D.P.
*D.P.
GAME No.
WMON RADIO MUNGE /NEW CASTLE

ROSE HITS IN 38 STRAIGHT TO BREAK NATIONAL
LEAGUE RECORD PREVIOUSLY HELD BY TOMMY HOLMES BOSTON BRAVES
IN [1945] HIT A 1 & 1 PITCH, PITCHER CRAIG SWAN.

Best Wishes   Pete Rose

EARL D. ARNOLD PRINTING CO., Cincinnati, Ohio

Scorecard from the game in which Pete Rose broke Tommy Holmes's consecutive-game National League hitting streak by hitting in his 38th straight game, July 25, 1978. He went on to hit in 44 straight before being stopped. Rose signed this scorecard after the game. (National Baseball Library, Cooperstown, N.Y.)

(2131) RIPKEN.

WEDNESDAY, SEPTEMBER 6, 1995 / Attendance 46,272

NO.	ANGELS	POS.	1	2	3	4	5	6	7	8	9	10	11	AB	R	H	RBI	E
19	Phillips	3B	F5	K			4-3	K						4	0	0	0	1
25	Edmonds	CF	8	7			BB							3	1	1	0	0
15	Salmon	RF	◆		/	K	•							4	1	3	2	0
44	Davis	DH	K		6-3 DP	BB	K							3	0	0	0	0
6	Snow	1B	8			7		K						4	0	1	0	0
16	Anderson, G	LF	7	K		7	3-1							4	0	0	0	0
10	Hudler	2B	K		7									2	0	0	0	0
14	Fabregas	C		63	43	K								3	0	0	0	0
1	EASLEY	SS		7										2	0	1	0	0
17	OWEN	PH/1B				5-3	8							2	0	0	0	0
	O. Palmiero	PH				4								1	0	0	0	0
	Correia	SS												0	0	0	0	0
	TOTALS		R 1	0	0	2	0	0	0	1	0			2	6	2	1	
			H 0	0	1	2	0	0	0	2								

NO.	ORIOLES	POS.	1	2	3	4	5	6	7	8	9	10	11	AB	R	H	RBI	E
9	Anderson, B	CF	F3	/	K	K								4	0	1	0	0
6	Alexander	2B	K	3	7	5-3								4	0	0	0	0
25	R. Palmeiro	1B	◆	9	/	◆								4	2	3	2	0
26	Bonilla	RF	K	◆	E-5	7								4	1	1	1	0
8	Ripken	SS	2	◆ 8	/									4	1	2	1	0
3	Baines	DH		7	K	K								4	0	1	0	0
23	Hoiles	C	5-1	5	/	8								4	0	1	0	0
30	Huson	3B		4	6	7								4	0	0	0	0
34	SMITH	LF		4	BB K									2	0	0	0	0
	J. BROWN	RF												0	0	0	0	0
	TOTALS		R 1	0	0	2	0	0	1	0	X			4	7	4	0	
			H 1	1	1	2	0	1	1	0								

1ST inn HR → SPECTACULAR TRY BY B. Anderson IN/OUT glove

CELEBRATION AT M. SMITH AB – SMITH 12 YRS OLD WHEN STREAK BEGAN

TEMP @ GAME TIME 89°

TIME OF GAME 3 hours, 36 minutes plus 22 minute delay in 5th for celebration that CAL Ripken Jr's record of 2,131 consecutive games was official.

Scorecard from Cal Ripken's record-breaking 2,131st straight game, September 6, 1995, vs. the California Angels. Scored by the author.

101

Scorecard for a game played among American servicemen on Tinian Island in the Pacific, August 26, 1945. The men divided themselves into American and National League teams, and each player appears to have affiliated himself with a favorite city or team. (National Baseball Library, Cooperstown, N.Y.)

Acknowledgments

These are the people who helped with the project and to whom I offer thanks:

Debbie Adkins; Paul Adomites; Michael Bojanowski of Chicago, whose files now contain the scorecards for over 1,200 major league games; John S. Bowman; Bob Brown of the Baltimore Orioles and the *Orioles Gazette*; Joe Castiglione; Stan Cohen; David Cataneo of the Boston *Herald*; Tom Dalzell for encouragement; Morris Eckhouse, executive director of SABR; Nelson Eddy; Kenneth Forehand; announcer and "Voice of Major League Baseball" Warner Fusselle; James L. Gates, Jr., librarian, National Baseball Hall of Fame; Craig Gerber of the California Angels; George Gibson; Bill Gilbert, editor, *The Diamond*; Steve Gietschier of *The Sporting News*; Bill Glasco; David Gordon; Joe Goulden; Dan Gutman; Jim Hall; Michael Hardcastle; Frederick Ivor-Campbell of the Society for American Baseball Research (SABR) Nineteenth Century Committee; Chuck Johnson; Dick Johnson and The Sports Museum of New England; Dave Kaplan, the New York *Daily News*; Dave Kelly, sports specialist at the Library of Congress; Michael Lackey of the Lima (Ohio) *News*; Thomas F. Larwin, president, San Diego Ted Williams Chapter of Society for American Baseball Research (SABR); Matthew E. Lieff; Skip McAfee; P. W. Maddrell of L. L. Bean; Bob Mayer; Ron Menchine, "baseball's greatest collector"; Kenneth B. Miller; Jeff Moder; Ray "the Voice of Softball" Molphy; Russell Mott; Ed Munson, California Angels official scorer; Joseph M. Overfield; Mark D. Pankin; William Plummer III, Amateur Softball Association; Michael B. Readdy; Tony Regitano, Onondaga Community College; David F. Riggs; Randy Roberts of the Western Historical Manuscript Collection at the University of Missouri; Joseph St. George; Tom Shieber; David Shulman; Jim Small, Office of the Commissioner; David W. Smith of Retrosheet, Newark, Delaware; Bob Staples, Mainely Sports, East Wilton, Maine; Chuck Thompson; Dean Vogelaar of the Kansas City Royals; Tim Wendell, major league editor, *USA Today Baseball Weekly*; Bob Wilson; and Al Yellon.

It should be noted that the basic system suggested at the beginning of the book is based on the good work and help of many individuals and relies heavily on systems long employed by Bob Brown, formerly of the Baltimore Orioles and the *Orioles Gazette*, and by announcer/writer Warner Fusselle.

Brown, who learned his system as a kid, taught it to the Oriole staff thirty years ago so that there would be uniformity in the team's recordkeeping, while Fusselle has seen his simple system become more and more sophisticated over the years. Special thanks to both.

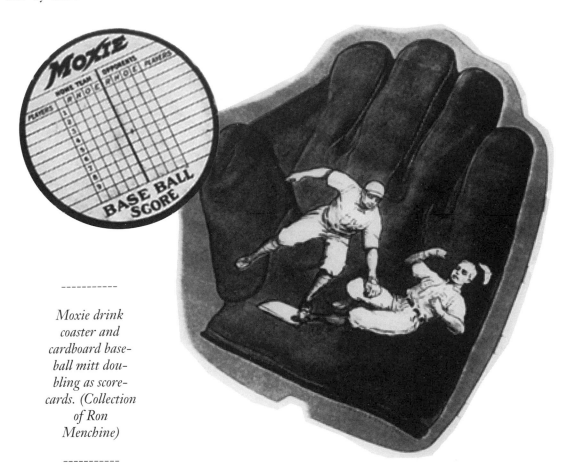

Moxie drink coaster and cardboard baseball mitt doubling as scorecards. (Collection of Ron Menchine)

Bibliography

"You can look it up," he'll say to doubters. They do and doubt no longer.
—REFERENCE TO CASEY STENGEL,
NEW YORK TIMES, OCTOBER 19, 1960

Addie, Bob. *Sportswriter*. Accent Publishing Inc., Lanham, Maryland, 1980.

Allen, Ethan. *Baseball: Major League Technique and Tactics*. The Macmillan Company, New York, 1953.

Allen, Mel. "Something New in Baseball," *This Week* magazine, July 11, 1954.

Alvarez, Mark. *The Old Ball Game*. Redefinition (The World of Baseball), Alexandria, Va., 1990.

Amateur Softball Association. *Scorer's Manual*. ASA, Oklahoma City, 1992.

Ames, Allen P. "How to Keep a Baseball Score." *St. Nicholas* magazine, June 1904 (694–7).

Angell, Roger. *Once More Around the Park*. Ballantine Books, New York, 1991.

Bartlett, Arthur Charles. *Baseball and Mr. Spalding*. Farrar, Straus and Young, New York, 1951.

Bean, L. L. *L. L. Bean's Simplified Baseball Score Book*. L. L. Bean, Freeport, Maine, 1954.

Boswell, Thomas. "The Scorecard," Boston Sunday *Globe*, September 23, 1979.

Bowman, John Stewart, and Joel Zoss. *Diamonds in the Rough: The Untold History of Baseball*. Macmillan, New York, 1989.

Brady, Erik. "Scorer's Rule: It's important to get it right." *USA Today*, July 10, 1990.

Broeg, Bob. "Official Scoring Not for Faint of Heart," *The Sporting News*, June 3, 1978.

Brosnan, Jim. *The Long Season*. Harper & Row, New York, 1975.

———. " 'X' in the Box Score," *New York Times Magazine*, September 10, 1961.

Butterfield, Fox. "Cooperstown? Hoboken? Try New York City," *New York Times*, October 4, 1990.

Castle, George. "Deciphering Baseball Hieroglyphics," *Chicago Cubs Official Souvenir Program and Scorecard*, Vol. 7, Number 3, 1988.

Chadwick, Henry, 1824–1908. [Base ball manual for 1871] *Chadwick's base ball manual for 1871*: containing the revised rules of the game for the season of 1871, also the new constitution and by-laws of the National Association of Amateur Base Ball Players, together with a history of the rise and progress of the old National Association, and a full detailed report of the proceedings of the two conventions of 1871: together with special articles on the newest points in pitching, batting, and fielding, also, records of principal clubs for 1869 and 1870, by Henry Chadwick. —New York: American News Co., 1871.

Charlton, James. *The Baseball Chronology: The Complete History of the Most Important Events in the Game of Baseball*. Macmillan, New York, 1991.

Cochrane, Gordon Stanley. *Baseball, the Fans' Game*. Funk & Wagnalls, New York, 1939.

Cohen, Neil. *The Official Baseball Hall of Fame Scorebook*. Little Simon, New York, 1989.

Cook, Earnshaw, in collaboration with Wendell R. Garner. *Percentage Baseball*. The M.I.T. Press, Cambridge, Mass.

Cosgrave, John Paul. *Cosgrave's Symbol Score-Book for Baseball Games*. Stockton Mail Publishing House, Stockton, California, 1887.

Couzens, Gerald Secor. *A Baseball Album*. Lippincott & Crowell, New York, 1980.

Cummings, Joseph Merriken. *How to Score; a practical textbook for scorers of base ball games, amateur and expert*. American Sports Publishing Company, New York, 1915, 1917, 1919.

Davids, L. Robert. *Insider's Baseball: The Finer Points of the Game, as Examined by the Society for American Baseball Research*, Scribner's, New York, 1983.

Day, Laraine. *Day With the Giants*. Doubleday, New York, 1952.

Dickson, Paul. *Baseball's Greatest Quotations*. Edward Burlingame Books (Harper Collins), New York, 1991.

———. *The Dickson Baseball Dictionary*. Facts on File, New York, 1989.

DiClerico, James M., and Barry J. Pavelec. *The Jersey Game*. Rutgers University Press, New Brunswick, N.J., 1991.

DiMaggio, Joe. *Baseball for Everyone*. Whittlesey House (McGraw-Hill), New York, 1948. (This book contains an appendix by Red Barber titled "How to Score.")

Dittmar, Joe. *Baseball's Benchmark Boxscores: Summaries of the record-setting games*, by Joseph J. Dittmar. Jefferson, N.C.: McFarland, 1990.

Durant, John. *The Story of Baseball in Words and Pictures*. Hastings House, New York, 1973.

Edelson, Mat. "E-Mom," *Outside Pitch*, June 10, 1994.

Einstein, Charles. *The Third Fireside Book of Baseball*, with an introduction by Stan Musial. Simon and Schuster, New York, 1968.

———. *The Fireside Book of Baseball*, 4th ed., edited by Charles Einstein; with an introduction by Reggie Jackson. Simon & Schuster, New York, 1987.

———. "Simplified Scoring," *Baseball Digest*, February 1969.

Falls, Joe. "The Unofficial Side of Official Scoring," *Baseball Digest*, August 1965.

Fiffer, Steve. *How to Watch Baseball*. Facts on File, New York, 1987.

Fimrite, Ron., ed. *Birth of a Fan*. Macmillan Pub. Co., New York, 1993.

Finch, Frank. "Is Scorer's Job a Joyride? Far From It!" *The Sporting News*, May 18, 1963.

Findlay, Jeri L. *Beyond the Basics of Scoring Fastpitch Softball*. Ball State University, Muncie, Indiana, 1990.

Fountain, Charles. *Sportswriter*. Oxford University Press, New York, 1993.

Freed, Doug. "Keeping Score." *Rocky Mountain News*, June 5, 1994.

Frick, Ford C. *Games, Asterisks, and People: Memoirs of a Lucky Fan*. Crown Publishers, New York, 1973.

Friedman, Arthur, and Joel H. Cohen. *The World of Sports Statistics: How the Fans and Professionals Record, Compile and Use Information*. Atheneum, New York, 1978.

Frommer, Harvey. *Primitive Baseball: The First Quarter-century of the National Pastime*. Atheneum, New York, 1988.

Fusselle, Warner. *Baseball—A Laughing Matter!* The Sporting News Pub. Co., St. Louis, 1987.

Gammon, Wirt. "Official Scorers Have to Field Some Bad Hops, Too," *Baseball Digest*, September 1963.

Giamatti, A. Bartlett. *Take Time for Paradise: Americans and their Games*. Summit Books, New York, 1989.

Glasco, Bill. *The Scorekeeper's Friend*. Published by William R. Glasco (P. O. Box 520241), Independence, Mo. 64052.

Goldstein, Warren Jay. *Playing for Keeps: A History of Early Baseball*. Cornell University Press, Ithaca, 1989.

Gould, James M. "Why Not Make Official Scoring More Official?", *Baseball Magazine*, March 1930.

Groff, D. Oscar, *The Official Base Ball Schedule for the Southern Association and National League with a Score Card*. Morning News, Savannah, 1894.

Hall, Donald. *Fathers Playing Catch with Sons: Essays on Sport, Mostly Baseball*. North Point Press, San Francisco, 1985.

Hano, Arnold. *A Day in the Bleachers*. Da Capo Press, New York, [1982], 1955.

Hawkins, Jim. "Official Scorers Have a Thankless Job," *Baseball Digest*, August, 1978.

———. "So You Want to Be An Official Scorer," *The Complete Handbook of Baseball*, 1979.

Henderson, Robert William. *Ball, Bat and Bishop: The Origin of Ball Games*. Rockport Press, New York, 1947.

Hernandez, Keith, and Mike Bryan. *Pure Baseball: Pitch by Pitch for the Advanced Fan*. HarperCollins, New York, 1994.

Higgins, H. Joseph. *Scoring a Baseball Game Play by Play*. City Baseball League, Kingsport, Tenn., 1934.

Hill, Art. *I Don't Care If I Never Come Back*. Simon and Schuster, New York, 1980.

Jones, Robert E. "Scoring Every Inning," *Baseball Research Journal*, X, 1981, 126–131.

Kahn, Roger, with Al Helfer. *The Mutual Baseball Almanac*. Doubleday and Co., New York, 1954.

Kaplan, Jim. "Do They Really Know the Score?" *Sports Illustrated*, July 24, 1978.

Kingston, John. *505 Baseball Questions Your Friends Can't Answer*. Walker and Co., New York, 1980.

Koppett, Leonard. *All About Baseball*. Quadrangle, New York, 1974.

Lackey, Mike. "Learning the Language of Summer: It's as Simple as 6-4-3," The Lima *News*, April 7, 1991.

Lang, Jack. "Writers Stumping for 'Team Error,'" *The Sporting News*, July 25, 1970.

Levine, Peter. *A. G. Spalding and the Rise of Baseball: The Promise of American Sport*. Oxford University Press, New York, 1985.

Lieb, Frederick G. *Baseball as I Have Known It*. Coward, McCann & Geoghegan, New York, 1977.

———. *How to Score*. The Sporting News, St. Louis, 1939, 1946.

Lindop, Edmund, and Joseph Jares. *White House Sportsmen*. Houghton Mifflin, Cambridge, 1964.

Lyttle, Richard. *The Official Baseball Scoreboard Book*. Wanderer Books (Simon and Schuster), New York, 1982.

Mack, Connie. *Connie Mack's Baseball Book*. Knopf, New York, 1950.

———. *My 66 Years in the Big Leagues*. John C. Winston Company, New York, 1950.

Mann, Arthur. *How to Play Winning Baseball*. Grossett and Dunlap, New York, 1953.

Marazzi, Richard. *The Rules and Lore of Baseball*. Stein and Day, New York, 1980.

McAnn, Richard. "It's a Hit—or Is It?", *For Men*, August 1939.

McKeever, Jim. "Scorekeepers Paint Baseball by the Numbers," Newhouse News Service, June 6, 1994.

Mead, William B., and Paul Dickson. *Baseball: The Presidents' Game*. Farragut Publishing Co., Washington, D.C., 1993.

Mead, William B. *The Inside Game*. Redefinition (The World of Baseball), Alexandria, Va., 1991.

Murnane, Timothy Hayes. *How to Score a Baseball Game*. American Sports Publishing Company, New York, Various editions 1907–1915.

Nelson, Lindsey. *Hello Everybody, I'm Lindsey Nelson*. Beech Tree Books (William Morrow), New York, 1985.

Nemec, David. *The Rules of Baseball*. Lyons & Burford, New York, 1994.

Okrent, Daniel. *Nine Innings*. Ticknor and Fields, New York, 1985.

Patterson, Arthur E. "Stevens Family, Caterers to Fans, Sold First Hot Dog on a Cold Day at Polo Grounds, 40 Years Ago," *The Sporting News*, November 23, 1939.

Povich, Shirley. *All These Mornings*. Prentice Hall, Englewood Cliffs, N.J., 1969.

Pozenel, John. "Knowing Score Fulltime Job for ISC Stats Man," Saginaw *News*, August 22, 1981.

Rebackoff, Zach. *Tough Calls*. Avon, New York, 1984.

Richards, Jack W., and Danny Hill. *Complete Handbook of Sports Scoring and Record Keeping*. Parker Publishing, Englewood Cliffs, N.J., 1974.

Rickey, Branch. *The American Diamond: A Documentary of the Game of Baseball*. Simon and Schuster, New York, 1965.

Salisbury, Luke. *The Answer Is Baseball*. Vintage, New York, 1990.

Sanders, Anthony. "In Baseball, It's Not Official Until the Scorer Makes the Call," *Cardinals Magazine*, August 1992.

Schlossberg, Dan. *The Baseball Catalog*. Jonathan David Publishers, Middle Village, N.Y., 1980.

Schwed, Fred Jr. *How to Watch a Baseball Game*. Harper and Brothers, New York, 1957.

Sexton, Joe. "Big Brother Isn't Watching, but Foote Is," *New York Times*, March 28, 1993.

Smith, Curt. *Voices of the Game*. Diamond Communications, South Bend, Ind., 1987.

Smith, H. Allen. "Some Baseball Statistics Anyone?", *Sports Illustrated*, January 9, 1956, 36–37.

Smith, Ira L., and H. Allen Smith. *Low and Inside*. Doubleday and Company, New York, 1949.

Duke Snider, with Bill Gilbert. *The Duke of Flatbush*. Introduction by Carl Erskine. Kensington Pub. Corp., New York, 1988.

Spink, C. C. Johnson. "Enjoyment for Everyone," *The Sporting News*, April 20, 1974.

Spink, J. G. Taylor. *The Sporting News Dope Book*. Charles C. Spink & Son (The Sporting News Publishing Co.), St. Louis, 1959.

Stack, C. P. "The Pleasure and Profit of Keeping Score," *Baseball Magazine*, M, May, 1914.

Stevens, Howell. "Scorers Can't Please Everybody," *Baseball Digest*, August 1948, 37–40.

Thorn, John. *The Armchair Book of Baseball*. Scribner's, New York, 1985.

———. *The Armchair Book of Baseball II*. Scribner's, New York, 1987.

———, and Pete Palmer with Michael Gershman. *Total Baseball*, 3rd ed. HarperPerennial, New York, 1993.

Waggoner, Glen, Kathleen Moloney, and Hugh Howard. *Baseball by the Rules: An Anecdotal Guide to America's Oldest and Most Complex Sport*. Taylor Pub. Co., Dallas, 1987.

Walter, Bucky. "Every Man His Own Scorekeeper—or How to Do It," *San Francisco News-Call Bulletin*, August 15, 1959.

Wolff, Bob. *Bob Wolff's Official Box Score Book*. 1948.

Wright, Harry. *The Official Score Book*. A. J. Reach, Wright and Ditson, New York, 1890. (Harry Wright's System.)

Young, Dick. "Young Ideas," *The Sporting News*, August 19, 1978.

Index